UNLOCKING THE MASONIC CODE: THE SECRET OF THE SOLOMON KEY

Ian Gittins

D1059904

Collins

For Mum and Dad

'May Freedom, Harmony and Love
Unite you in the grand Design
Beneath th'Omniscient Eye above
The glorious Architect Divine'

Robert Burns, The Farewell
to the Brethren of St James
Lodge, Tarbolton (1786)

First published in 2007 by Collins,
an imprint of HarperCollins Publishers
77-85 Fulham Palace Road
Hammersmith
London w6 8jb

The Collins website address is www.collins.co.uk

Collins is a registered trademark of HarperCollins Publishers Ltd

Text © 2007 Ian Gittins
Internal illustrations © 2007 Cara Wilson

isbn-10: 0-00-723467-8
isbn-13: 978-0-00-723467-7

A catalogue record for this book is
available from the British Library.

Typeset by Rowland Phototypesetting Ltd,
Bury St Edmunds, Suffolk

Printed and bound in Clays Ltd, St Ives plc

This book is proudly printed on paper which contains wood
from well managed forests, certified in accordance with
the rules of the Forest Stewardship Council.
For more information about FSC,
please visit www.fsc-uk.org

CONTENTS

INTRODUCTION   1

1. THE REAL HISTORY OF
   FREEMASONRY   15

2. THE NOTIONAL HISTORY OF
   FREEMASONRY:
   GREAT CONSPIRACY THEORIES   75

3. INSIDE THE LODGE:
   MASONIC RITUALS AND
   SYMBOLS   124

4. MASONIC SYMBOLS –
   A BRIEF GUIDE   221

5. FAMOUS FREEMASONS   232

INDEX   248

INTRODUCTION

The pseudo-historical fiction of Dan Brown is the publishing phenomenon of the first few years of the twenty-first century. By early 2005, over twenty-five million copies of *The Da Vinci Code*, the Gordian knot of a detective novel that saw Harvard Professor Robert Langdon in learned pursuit of the Holy Grail, were in print around the globe. Brown's intricate weaving of mysticism, alternative history and cryptic symbolism into a good old-fashioned pot-boiler clearly touched a nerve in the worldwide popular consciousness.

As the year progressed, and with a Ron Howard-directed Hollywood movie of *The Da Vinci Code* starring Tom Hanks and Audrey Tatou at an advanced stage of production, Brown acolytes speculated over what the author's next move would be. Countless *Da Vinci Code*-fixated chat rooms and fansites hummed with chatter and speculation. At which point, with *The Da Vinci*

Code's worldwide sales up to forty million, Brown himself revealed exactly where he would be directing Langdon next – into the dark heart of Freemasonry.

Writing on his own website, www.danbrown. com, the author had this to say about the legendarily secretive Masons: 'My interest sparks from growing up in New England, surrounded by the clandestine clubs of Ivy League universities, the Masonic lodges of our Founding Fathers, and the hidden hallways of early government power.' His next novel, *The Solomon Key*, would, he confirmed, be set 'deep within the oldest fraternity in history – the enigmatic brotherhood of the Masons.'

In truth, it is not terribly difficult to comprehend the appeal of Freemasonry to Brown in a novelistic context. His books are labyrinthine riddles, set in a world of proscribed societies, arcane and complex symbolism and historical facts and suppositions woven into the sort of beguiling conspiracy theories that invariably attract eager adherants. What could suit his creative purposes better than a mysterious, ancient fraternal society with its own mythology founded on an opaque system of secret symbols, rituals and handshakes?

Broadly speaking, there are two schools of thought on the Masons. The first – grounded in reality, and therefore of little use to Brown – is that the Freemasons are a modern anachronism, an eccentric but essentially benign organization of men whose well-developed sense of self-importance is a minor flaw compared to the many good charitable works that they do. This view holds that, given the increasing average age of the membership, the fraternity is unlikely to survive in any significant form beyond the next two or three decades.

The rival opinion, and the one seized upon by Brown, is that the Freemasons are a shadowy grouping of sinister malcontents bent on subverting society and possibly – eventually – achieving world domination. The more turbo-charged conspiracy theorists out there even argue that the organization is in possession of ancient mystical secrets, of a sacred or even occult nature, handed down to them by the Knights Templar, the famous chapter of medieval warrior knights.

The more pathologically driven detractors

point towards the significant role played by Masons in the birth of America – many of the Founding Fathers were Freemasons, as was the first President, George Washington – and imply that the fraternity, even today, still enacts a Machiavellian influence at the very apex of politics and the worlds of finance and business. Such loaded theorizing, naturally, is manna from heaven to a novelist as shrewd as Dan Brown as he sets about weaving a work of charged fiction like *The Solomon Key*.

So, are the Freemasons a bunch of harmless old duffers indulging in a little fanciful role-playing – essentially, Britain's Rotary Club or America's Elks with their trouser-legs rolled up – or are they mystical, scheming figures with powers and knowledge beyond the ken of the uninitiated? To gain a little insight, let's begin by examining the organization's philosophy and *modus operandi*.

What is Freemasonry?

Frequently described as a 'peculiar system of morality veiled in allegory and illuminated by symbols', Freemasonry remains the largest and most high-profile/notorious secular fraternal society in the world. While it is known to have descended from the stonemasons' guilds of medieval times, as we shall explain in depth in Chapter 1: The Real History of Freemasonry, some argue that its lineage extends right back to the time of King Solomon – a deeply tenuous claim, but one that we shall examine in greater depth later in this book.

Few dispute that Freemasonry is in decline, with the fraternity's membership numbers consistently dropping since the Sixties. Nevertheless, it remains a formidable organization. There are still more than five million Masons worldwide – four million of them in the United States, 500,000 in England and Wales, slightly under 400,000 in Scotland, and significant numbers in France, Canada, Australia and Ireland, as well as smaller but active chapters in Latin America, India, Japan, the Philippines and Israel.

At heart – leaving aside, for a second, its complex and intimidating historical provenance – Freemasonry is a benevolent philosophical movement. Members are taught to develop their character and altruistic instincts via a series of catechisms and ritual dramas, through which they progress through the fraternity until they are initiated as a Master Mason. The rituals and ceremonies are so arcane – and we shall detail them in full later in the book – that one almost suspects the movement's legendary secrecy is intended primarily to save them from the howls of mockery of the outside world.

Yet setting such scepticism temporarily aside, the Masons' motivations are largely noble ones. Initiates are told to cherish and propound the three central tenets of brotherly love, charity towards fellow Masons and the wider world, and truth. On a purely practical level, there is no denying the good works carried out by the fraternity: it is estimated that British Masons spend around £3 million per year on charitable projects. In America, the figure is nearer to $1 billion.

The Masons have suffered a degree of ridicule in recent decades due to the impenetrable rituals and extraordinary ceremonies that have defined the movement in the public imagination. Their formalities can seem ludicrously exclusive and laughably pompous. Dan Brown possibly deserves a degree of grudging recognition for his achievement in making a centuries-old, arcane grouping of pensioners and retirees appear like a dangerous and intimidating global force blessed/burdened with mystical secrets and knowledge.

Although its roots are in Christianity, the Freemasons (or 'the Craft' as it is often known) are a determinedly secular gathering. Members are required to pledge allegiance to a Supreme Being, but there is no obligation specifically to identify this deity as the Christian God, Allah or Buddha. During all Masonic meetings or ceremonies, this Supreme Being is referred to as the Grand Architect Of The Universe – a non-denominational philosophy that has led Masonry to be condemned by most major religions at some point in its eventful history.

Freemasons meet at regular intervals – normally once per month – in a local headquarters known as a lodge. Although these buildings are sometimes made available to the public for non-Masonic activities, they all contain an inner sanctum ritual area, laid out in a highly defined fashion and decorated with elaborate symbols, in which meetings and degree ceremonies are held. These areas are out of bounds to cynics, the curious and non-Masons in general.

Each local lodge is affiliated to a Grand Lodge, a regional over-body that serves as an administrative and legislative centre for the affiliate lodges. Yet this is about as coherent as the Craft gets. Inconveniently for Dan Brown and his fellow conspiracy theorists, there is no over-arching international body in charge of global Freemasonry: indeed, a history of various political and philosophical differences means that many Grand Lodges fail even to acknowledge each other's existence. One is put in mind more of bickering parish councils than a furtive secret order hell-bent on establishing a self-serving New World Order.

The potential for international sedition is handicapped even further by the fact that Masons are not allowed to discuss religion, politics or any other traditionally divisive subject while inside the confines of the lodge. Nor is there any consideration of an after-life. Freemasons' energies are directed entirely towards self-improvement on earth, a dogged quest for spiritual perfection towards which they proceed in regulated, formalized degrees.

How do you join the Freemasons?

The idea of exclusivity and covertness that surrounds the Masons is now largely a myth. Any male over twenty-one and with no criminal record who approaches a lodge is likely to be admitted. Existing members vote on whether the applicant should be allowed to join, but only in exceptional circumstances nowadays are people refused. With membership numbers falling, Masonic lodges are in desperate need of fresh blood.

Once the applicant is accepted, he educates himself in Freemasonry's history and philosophy and is tested on his learning via a series of ritualistic degree ceremonies. These bizarre role-playing exercises – wherein the initiate is blind-folded, led by a rope and has his trouser-legs and shirt-sleeves rolled up – is the limit of most people's casual knowledge of the Masons, and leads to the common perception of the fraternity as being slightly less relevant to the modern world than the Flat Earth Society.

The initiate also learns a series of signs (passwords) and grips (handshakes) by which he can secretly make himself known to fellow Masons when they meet in public. These arcane relics of medieval days are the only facet of Freemasonry that the movement still tries to keep secret. Nevertheless, anti-Masonic militants have for years splashed this information over various anti-cult websites, and we shall also divulge this hallowed information at the appropriate point in this book (*see* Chapter 3: Inside The Lodge: Masonic Rituals and Symbols).

The three degrees that a Freemason travels through on his path to spiritual enlightenment are:

- Entered Apprentice – the man is initiated into the lodge and swears allegiance to the Craft;
- Fellow Craft – having proven himself willing and able, the member is given extra knowledge and responsibilities;
- Master Mason – once he has reached this 'supreme and exalted rank', the Mason becomes a leading light of the lodge.

* * * * * * * *

Men Only

Like the Great Room at Lord's, Freemasonry remains a last bastion of male chauvinism. Masonry was a male-only province until 1877, when maverick French Grand Lodge the Grand Orient de France horrified traditionalist Masons by admitting female members. This led to the French body being ostracized by most of the movement, and today both English and US Masonry's controlling bodies refuse to admit women. Yet there are a few female lodges in England that are grudgingly semi-recognized by the United Grand Lodge of England (UGLE), who in 1999 confirmed 'Freemasonry is not confined to men' before hastily adding, 'This Grand Lodge itself does not admit women'.

* * * * * * * *

Particularly zealous Freemasons can collect further honours by taking the additional degrees of the York Rite and Scottish Rite – the latter discipline allows them to pursue no fewer than thirty-two levels of Masonic education and enlightenment. However, these 'appendant' degrees are optional, and theoretically even a 32nd degree Scottish Rite Mason is in no way superior to a common-or-garden Master Mason.

The names of the three main degrees awarded to Freemasons, and the phraseology used within the ceremonies, take their cue from the language used by the working stonemasons of the Middle Ages. These hugely gifted craftsmen made use of geometry and supreme architectural skills to build the soaring Gothic cathedrals whose very existence supposedly proved the glory of God. Their structures were viewed as a divine perfection on Earth.

As we shall see later in this book, Freemason philosophy likens the soul of every Mason to such an edifice. It is the task of the Freemason to improve himself morally and spiritually, through rite, ritual and a fundamental understanding of the world around him, until he aspires to a state of human perfection. Yet this perfection is viewed as the work of a Supreme Being – which is why atheists are not allowed to become Masons.

Wild-eyed anti-Masonic jihadists (and Dan Brown) may speculate about Freemasonry as a demonic, sinister cabal, but most modern objections to the movement are more workaday and prosaic. Outsiders have long considered the Freemasons to be an old boys' club whose members will invariably do each other favours outside of the lodge. This view has been supported by various scandals over the years, including a damaging late 1970s court case in which senior London High Court judges, police chiefs and pornographers were implicated. It may not be the Knights Templar, but such corruption does the fraternity's public relations image few favours.

Masonry's riposte to this charge is that such nepotism is forbidden by statute. Freemasons are barred under the movement's laws, or 'Charges', from using their membership to promote their own interests, or from extending cronyism to fellow lodge members. Theoretically, such lapses are punishable by expulsion from the fraternity, although it is reasonable to suspect that the handful of cases that have been discovered over the years represent the tip of the iceberg.

Nor are Freemasons particularly secretive nowadays. Beyond the signs, grips and precise ceremonies, the organization is largely an open book. Anybody wishing to approach their local Grand Lodge to discuss becoming a Mason will find their number in the telephone directory. In America, where they have always done things rather differently, lodges have even run billboard campaigns to attempt to boost their membership.

So with global Freemasonry in decline and its social significance and power arguably at it lowest point in centuries, what makes Dan Brown think the Craft is a fitting setting for the latest convoluted and faintly preposterous adventures of Robert Langdon? To answer that question, let's examine the two parallel histories of Freemasonry – the real one, and the fanciful version that has over the years fuelled the imaginative fantasies of so many conspiracy theorists and exploitative opportunists.

1

THE REAL HISTORY OF FREEMASONRY

The casual observer may be perplexed that Dan Brown finds the need to play historical hopscotch and concoct an alternative provenance for the Freemasons, as the colourful and vibrant history of the much-maligned movement is fascinating in its own right. Over the years the Masons have found themselves the enemies of kings, popes, dictators and democrats alike – there are few periods in history when the organization has not aroused fear and suspicion. Having survived the Inquisition and Nazi persecution, it's safe to say that Freemasonry is unlikely to regard an assault by a pulp fiction novelist, albeit a highly successful one, as its darkest hour.

The practical roots of Freemasonry lie in the stonemasons' guilds formed by working masons from the twelfth century on. However, its philosophical base is grounded far deeper – in the construction of King Solomon's Temple on the sacred land of Mount Moriah, Jerusalem, in the tenth century BC by King David of Israel.

In Masonic lore, numerous rituals and ceremonies are based on King Solomon's Temple, and specifically on a particularly grisly murder that is said to have been committed there. It is worth examining the history and the fanciful fables that are attached to this biblical-era temple, as they have echoes in almost every branch and aspect of Freemasonry as it exists today.

The Building of King Solomon's Temple

Mount Moriah is one of the most controversial religious flashpoints on the face of the Earth. Three millennia on from King David's day, the locale – now known as Temple Mount – is vigorously claimed by both Judaism and Islam, and remains one of the largest stumbling blocks to a negotiated settlement between Israel and Palestine. When then-Israeli opposition leader Ariel Sharon visited the site, in September 2000, the hostile Arab response to his visit led to the uprising that became known as the al-Aqsa Intifada.

The site is cherished because the holy books of both faiths describe miraculous events happening there. The Bible identifies Mount Moriah as the place where God commanded Abraham to sacrifice his only son, Isaac. The Koran, for its part, claims that Mohammed climbed a golden ladder of light from this sacred rock to heaven, where Allah instructed him in the forms of worship and devotion to be followed by all Muslims.

Biblical legend has it that David conquered the people of Jebus in 1000 BC and established Jerusalem as Israel's capital city. The King intended to build a vast temple on Mount Moriah, but was forbidden to do so by God because of the copious bloody wars he had waged while on Israel's throne. David had also sent a loyal courtier, Uriah, to certain death in battle so that he could seduce his wife, Bathsheba. In 981 BC, she bore him a son – Solomon.

David remained fixated on building a temple on the mount, and before his death he collected vast resources to allow Solomon to perform the task – the Bible claims it to have been 100,000 talents (approx 3,000 tons) of gold and one million talents (300,000 tons) of silver. After his father's demise, Solomon commenced the construction process. As 1 Kings 5:5 has it:

Behold, I purpose to build a house unto the name of the Lord my God, as the Lord spake unto David my father, saying, Thy son, whom I will set upon thy throne in thy room, he shall build a house unto my name.

Feeling Israel did not have enough architects and skilled workers to take on the building of the temple, Solomon asked for help from Hiram I, the Phoenician King of Tyre. Hiram obliged, sending leading members of the ancient collective of builders known as the Dionysian Artificers of Tyre (see page 79) as well as thousands of labourers and thousands of tons of Lebanese timber. He also dispatched a man who was to become central to the narrative of the Freemasons – Hiram Abiff, Tyre's most gifted architect and mathematician.

Described in I Kings 7:14 as 'a widow's son ... a worker in brass ... filled with wisdom and understanding', Hiram Abiff oversaw the entire temple project, alongside King Solomon himself and

Hiram, King of Tyre. Work on the temple began in the fourth year of King Solomon's reign, 956 BC, and lasted for seven years. The largely Phoenician workforce built the edifice in the prevailing Phoenician or Egyptian style, which meant that a small outer vestibule, flanked by two ornate bronze pillars named Jachin and Boaz, led into a larger middle chamber. This transition room was known as *Hekal*, or Holy Place.

The centrepiece of the temple was the *Sanctum Sanctorum*, or Holiest of Holies, a windowless chamber that it is said was lined throughout with gold and Lebanese cedar. This central room was intended to house the Ark of the Covenant – the stone tablets passed by God to Moses on the Mount – a jar of manna and the Rod of Aaron – the staff carried by Moses' brother, which supposedly grew buds and bore fruit when Moses carried it into the Tabernacle (*see* Numbers 17:8). Only rabbis and holy men could enter these inner chambers of Solomon's Temple – non-ordained Jews worshipped outside the building.

It is believed that King Solomon's Temple was finished around 949–948 BC. Despite its striking design and glitteringly ornate interior, it was actually fairly small: 90 foot long by 30 foot wide and 45 foot tall. However, as this feat of ancient engineering was nearing completion, Masons believe that the genius architect over-seeing the process, Hiram Abiff, was brutally slain.

The Hiramic Legend:
The Murder of Hiram Abiff

It is – to say the least – a moot point whether a gifted early stonemason named Hiram Abiff was really killed at King Solomon's Temple. The Christian scriptures that detail the building of the temple make no reference to this occurrence, and nor do Islamic texts covering this period. Despite this, the murder has become a centrepiece of Masonic faith, education and ritual.

Freemason literature claims that Hiram Abiff, as well as being the chief designer and architect of the temple, supervised the project's prodigious workforce: beneath him, claims the Book of Kings, were 3,300 foremen and 150,000 masons and labourers. Solomon and the two Hirams are said to have divided these workers into three ranks, dependent on ability.

These levels were Entered Apprentice, Fellow of the Craft and Master Mason. The rates of pay increased as a worker improved his skills and was promoted, with a Master Mason being the most prestigious and best remunerated. Workers queuing to be paid by King Solomon's clerks would identify their rank by giving the wages clerk the secret password and sign that identified each level of employment.

One of Hiram Abiff's many duties was deciding which employees were ready to take on more onerous duties and be promoted to Fellow of the Craft or Master Mason. The chief architect set exacting standards and was notoriously hard to impress, and fifteen of his workers hatched a plot to confront Hiram Abiff and issue him with an ultimatum: either he promote them to the higher rank or they would beat, or even kill him.

Masonic legend has it that twelve of the conspirators got cold feet and dropped out. However, three of them – with the hugely unlikely, nursery rhyme-friendly names of Jubela, Jubelo and Jubelum – lay in wait at the three separate entrances of the *Sanctum Sanctorum*, and confronted Hiram Abiff as he left his customary midday private prayers.

Hiram Abiff emerged from the east door and was met by Jubela, who put his demand to be elevated to Master Mason. When Hiram Abiff refused, an irate Jubela slashed open his boss's throat with one of the tools of the Masonic trade – a 24-inch measuring gauge. Mortally wounded, Hiram Abiff staggered to the south door, where Jubelo attacked him with an architect's square. With the last strength in his body, he crawled to the west entrance, where Jubelum killed him with a blow to the head with a maul, or gavel.

Panicking, the murderers hid the chief architect's body in a quarry near to the Temple, returning hours later to bury him in a shallow grave – it was said to be six feet long, six feet wide and six feet deep – with a sprig of acacia on top. Having covered their tracks, they then fled Jerusalem and took refuge in a small Mediterranean town named Joppa.

The twelve conspirators who had backed out of the plan to confront Hiram Abiff went to see King Solomon the next day and confessed their conspiracy: in Masonic accounts of this incident, they wore white aprons as a sign that their own hands were free of blood. Solomon dispatched men in pursuit of Jubela, Jubelo and Jubelum, who were soon apprehended in Joppa.

The punishment of the killers is one of the most lurid flights of fancy in Masonic literature. It is claimed that when they were captured, all three men were crying out in horror at the crime they had committed: Jubela confessed an urge to have his throat cut and his tongue 'torn out by the root and buried in the sands of the sea at low water, a cable length from the shore'. Sharing his woe, Jubelo demanded that his heart be 'torn from under my naked left breast, and given to the vultures of the air as a prey'.

Having struck the fatal blow, Jubelum was the most contrite: his express wish was to have 'my body severed in two, one part carried to the south, and the other to the north, my bowels burnt to ashes and scattered before the four winds of the earth'. The three murderers had their gruesome wishes granted: exercising his fabled wisdom, King Solomon decreed that each of them should meet their sorry end exactly as they had predicted.

*   *   *   *   *   *   *   *

The Widow's Son

Masonic lore holds that Hiram Abiff's last words before he died were 'Is there no help for the widow's son?'. This phrase holds an extraordinary resonance in Freemasonry, and is used by Masons in distress to seek help from fellow members. Dan Brown indicated that *The Solomon Key* **would concern itself with Masonry by hiding the phrase in bold text on the front cover flap of** *The Da Vinci Code,* **then alerting readers to its existence via his website.**

*   *   *   *   *   *   *   *

After Hiram Abiff's death, King Solomon and Hiram of Tyre oversaw the completion of the project, but fate was not kind to their creation. After it had stood for four centuries on Mount Moriah, the Temple was demolished by King Nebuchadnezzar when he seized Israel for the Babylonians. The Babylonian forces sacked Jerusalem and burned the Temple and the entire city to the ground. The Temple treasures were looted – except for the Ark of the Covenant, which

had mysteriously vanished. (The quest for elements of this 'Holy Grail', of course, formed the
fulcrum of Dan Brown's *The Da Vinci Code*.)

After half a century of exile in Babylon, the Jews
returned to Israel and rebuilt King Solomon's
Temple under Zerubbabel in 520 BC. This structure fared little better than the original, being torn
down by the Romans in AD 70 when the Jews were
again banished from Israel.

Today, two of the holiest of Muslim edifices,
the al-Aqsa Mosque and the Dome on the Rock,
dominate Mount Moriah. The remains of the
foundations of King Solomon's Temple are known
as the Wailing Wall, and thousands of Jews
make pilgrimages there every year. Yet Solomon's
Temple lives on, bizarrely, in the arcane rituals
of a secretive fraternity that was to spring up in
Great Britain more than two millennia after Hiram
Abiff was purportedly killed – the Freemasons.

Medieval Masons

Two thousand years after King David supposedly
asked God for permission to build a temple in

Jerusalem, spectacular houses of worship were springing up right across western Europe. The Roman Catholic Church was at the peak of its dominance and empire-building, and a succession of popes ordered the building of a series of magnificent cathedrals to inspire awe and devotion in all who set eyes upon them – and, as a consequence, to cement the Church's own seemingly impregnable control over society.

The end of the eleventh century thus marked the arrival of Gothic architecture, the style whose majesty and opulence was intended to reflect the splendour and glory of an omnipotent God. This ornate school of architecture was first glimpsed in England and northern France, but by the middle of the twelfth century had spread through Germany and the Low Countries and as far south as Italy and Spain.

The Gothic style emphasized huge, towering vertical stone edifices that held enormous painted glass windows with ribbed vaults and pointed arches – the classic look of the medieval cathedral. These houses of worship were frequently decorated with statues on the outside, while the elaborate windows re-enacted Biblical stories –

visual aids that were highly useful given that the vast majority of the congregation in those days would have been completely illiterate.

The stunning architecture of these portentous structures mirrored exactly the theological messages spreading from Rome. God – and his representatives on earth, the Catholic Church – were all-powerful and almighty. The sky-scraping Gothic cathedrals were his power made concrete: the sole response demanded of the ordinary man was unquestioning supplication. The floor plan of these temples of worship invariably spelt out a cross.

It is perhaps unsurprising that these towering edifices seemed like living miracles to the uneducated serfs and labourers of medieval England. It was certainly difficult to comprehend how the slender columns that rose from the floor of the building could support the neck-craning ceilings and heavy ornamentation. The overwhelmed worshipper could be forgiven for assuming that only divine intervention held the whole structure in place.

The truth was a little more prosaic: Gothic cathedrals benefited from the design feature known as the flying buttress, a projecting structure that was built on the outside of the building to counter the gravitational thrust of the roof. These external supports removed the need for bulky stone pillars inside the church and facilitated the vast and resplendent stained-glass windows.

Just as these cloud-bursting wonders of medieval engineering seemed divinely inspired, so the men who designed and crafted them were regarded as miracle workers. The handful of Master Masons possessed of the skill in geometry, mathematics and physics to oversee such constructions were held in veneration by kings, church leaders and the hoi-polloi alike. Few posts outside of the royal court held greater social cachet, or were more widely coveted.

Initially Masons came under the theoretical control of the Masons' Livery Company, a regulatory body established in 1220 that sought to establish maximum fees, working conditions and guarantees of Godly behaviour upon Master Masons. Understandably profoundly un-impressed at these attempts to fix a low ceiling on their large earning potential, Masons reacted

* * * * * * * *

The origins of the term Freemason

There is no agreed absolute etymological derivation of the term Freemason but, rather, two competing theories. Medieval construction workers were divided into the labourers who cut the hard stones from the quarries (known as Rough Masons) and the skilled workmen who shaped the softer, more malleable rock known as free stone. These workers became known as Free Stone Masons, later shortened to Freemasons. A simpler explanation is that these Masons, freed from regular employment, were able to travel around the country looking for work, and thus were genuinely Free Masons.

* * * * * * * *

by creating their own stonemasons' trade guilds.

Part-educational college, part-fledgling trade union, these guilds were initially illegal and their members forced to convene in secret. Their dual goals were to train up future Master Masons in the skills of designing and erecting vast cathedrals, while at the same time zealously guarding the knowledge and tricks of the trade that enabled them to do so. To this end, members were given signs (passwords) and grips (handshakes) by which they could identify fellow Masons before sharing crucial information with them.

Furthermore, the guilds operated on a strictly hierarchical basis. Students admitted to the fraternity, who were often as young as twelve, were schooled both in theory and on the job by Master Masons. As these Masons continued their training they were allowed privileges along the way, such as the right to carve their own identifying 'mark' into some cathedral stones.

However, even the most gifted student was highly unlikely to become a Master Mason in less than ten years. Were he to divulge even the most minor trade secret to an outsider, he would be instantly banished from the guild and ostracized by all Master Masons.

As Church and State became aware of the existence of stonemasons' guilds, there were attempts to legislate them out of existence. In 1360, King Edward III passed a law banning all secret Masonic pledges and societies, and sixty-five years later the Regency Government forbade Masons to gather in numbers in any circumstances. This law was soon deemed unworkable and was rarely applied.

The twelfth to fourteenth centuries saw Freemasons scale new heights of influence and importance. As Gothic cathedrals sprang up across Europe, their services were in sharp demand. Masons rebuilt Canterbury Cathedral along Gothic lines in 1174 after its eastern wing was destroyed by fire. However, Wells Cathedral, where construction work began in 1180, is generally regarded as the first major English cathedral built entirely in the Gothic style.

Westminster Abbey, York Minster, Ely Cathedral and Winchester Cathedral all had Gothic devices added to their existing edifices, and across the Channel in France imposing structures arose at Notre-Dame in Paris, Chartres, Amiens and Rouen. Unsurprisingly, the Catholic Church also built cathedrals nearer to home, in Milan, Florence and Siena, as well as across the Low Countries and Spain.

Yet despite their elevated social and occupational status, Freemasons were largely far from venal and self-serving. The stonemasons' guilds may have been formed partly to protect their members' business interests, but these bodies also strove to inculcate high standards of moral and personal behaviour amongst practitioners of the trade. Various rules, or 'Charges', urged Masons to render their own lives as noble and upright as the cathedrals they built – not a concern that you can imagine troubling the labour unions of today.

The Regius Manuscript

The Regius Manuscript is one of the most significant documents in Masonic history. Presented to the British Museum by King George II in 1757, it was written in 1390, possibly by a priest, although numerous clues within the text suggest that it was copied from even earlier documents, possibly dating from around 950–1000 AD. Entitled 'A Poem of Moral Duties', this 794-line loosely rhyming piece of verse summarized the professional, moral and philosophical levels of behaviour expected of Masons, as well as making some extravagant and fanciful historical claims.

The Regius Manuscript (also called the Halliwell Manuscript after James Halliwell, who translated it from the original Old English in 1840) opens with a Latin inscription: *Hic incipiunt constitutiones artis gemetrioe secundum Euclydum*. Translating as 'Here begin the constitutions of geometry according to Euclid', the motto shows the importance given to the science of geometry in Masonic theory and ritual: after all, these precise calculations enabled the building of their trademark towering cathedrals.

This elongated meditation on spirituality and Masonry ('the most honest craft of all') opens with the claim that Euclid, in addition to inventing geometry, was also the first Master Mason and had, indeed, founded the entire Craft in ancient Egypt. Scarcely missing a beat, the poem goes on to claim that Freemasonry was imported to England by King Athelstan, who instigated Masonic meetings and 'loved this craft full well'.

The poem claims that King Athelstan called a vast meeting of Freemasons from the length of Britain, which was also attended by 'Lords in their state / Dukes, earls and barons too'. This august assembly drew up the rules and strictures that

* * * * * * * *

King Athelstan

The grandson of Alfred the Great, King Athelstan (895–939 AD) was the first king of all England. Taking York from the Danes, he also forced the surrender of King Constantine of Scotland, united Britain beneath his command and repelled all invasions. This otherwise little-celebrated historical figure occupies a crucial place in Masonic history.

The Regius Manuscript claims that King Athelstan was a keen supporter of Masonry and in 926 AD, one year after he came to the throne, called the very first Grand Lodge of Masons at York. Appointing his brother Edwin the Lodge Grand Master, he commanded it to convene annually thereafter, and also supported Freemasonry by commissioning a constant stream of new forts, castles and monasteries.

There is no doubt that Freemasonry's York Rite takes its cue from the Regius Manuscript and the supposed 926 AD York Assembly. It is likely, however, that the document adds a few imaginative flourishes to the actual contribution to Masonry of King Athelstan.

* * * * * * * *

were to govern the stonemasons' guilds, dividing them into fifteen regulatory 'articles' and a further fifteen philosophical 'points', and looked to correct 'defaults' that Athelstan had noted in Masons' work standards and general comportment.

The fifteen articles outline the basic requirements and responsibilities of a Master Mason. The first two explain that he should be honest ('as a judge stand upright'), reliable, and pay his workmen fairly and on time. He should also attend every meeting of his chapter of Masons, unless 'sickness hath him so strong / That he may not come them among'.

The majority of the articles thereafter deal with the relationship between the Master Mason and the Fellows of the Craft and Entered Apprentices beneath his command. The Mason should ensure that every apprentice is willing and able to study for seven years. He should not recruit a servant, lest his owner should remove him from service of the Craft, nor should he hire or initiate an apprentice who is 'deformed' or 'maimed' (in 1390, the more politically correct phrase 'physically challenged' clearly had yet to enter the lexicon).

The articles further inform the Mason not to recruit thieves, and swiftly to replace any Entered Apprentices who fall short of the Craft's high standards. The Master Mason should not accept commissions that he knows he cannot fulfil, nor steal work from a fellow Mason. Nor should he withhold any trade secrets from his apprentices, but rather ensure that he 'the craft ably may know / Wheresoever he go under the sun'.

The Regius Manuscript's fifteen 'points' are of a more general nature, urging the Masons towards serene and contemplative behaviour. The Mason must 'love God and holy church always / and his master also', be discreet, treat all men equally and receive his pay and rewards 'meekly'. He should also be a peace-maker and steer well clear of the 'foul deadly sin' of sleeping with a fellow Mason's wife. He should be a patriot ('To his liege lord the King ... be true to him over all thing') and, crucially, be willing to swear an oath of his commitment to the Craft before the Master Mason and fellow members.

The Manuscript then veers off into a fable of four Masons who refused to make monuments of false gods at the behest of a Roman emperor and so were martyred (see page 81), before re-capping Christian fables such as Noah's Ark and the Tower of Babel and identifying seven 'sciences' in which the civilized Mason should be adept: grammar, dialect, rhetoric, music, astronomy, arithmetic and geometry. The poem ends by reminding the Mason once again of the virtues of truth, honesty and humility.

The Regius Manuscript emphasizes that Middle Ages Masonry had its self-improvement and spiritual aspects, but nevertheless the stone-masons' guilds remained largely professional organizations-cum-trade unions. However, events at the start of the sixteenth century conspired to ensure that Freemasons would henceforth have far more time on their hands to consider matters of a more abstract, philosophical nature.

The 1500s saw Masonry hit with a devastating triple blow. Firstly, the Renaissance and the Age of Enlightenment meant it was harder for Masons to jealously guard their trade secrets. With the advent of the printing presses, Gothic cathedrals could no longer be seen as God-made-stone via divine powers: instead, the mechanics of the

* * * * * * * *

The Cooke Manuscript

The second most important medieval document in Freemasonry is the Cooke Manuscript, named after its 1861 translator and editor, Matthew Cooke. Written around 1450, this instructional tome was penned by a Mason rather that a priest, and contains many of the central pillars of Masonic lore. As well as describing the building of King Solomon's Temple, the manuscript also concerns itself with Masonic symbolism and ritual and was clearly highly influential on the philosophy and minutiae of modern Freemasonry.

* * * * * * * *

no-longer-mysterious flying buttress were laid bare for all to see.

As the Masons came to terms with no longer being workers of modern miracles, their chief patron was also in trouble. The Roman Catholic Church, for so long all-conquering across Europe, faced dissent wherever it turned, with Martin Luther sparking the Protestant Reformation in Germany in 1517 and King Henry VIII breaking all

British ties with Rome in 1534. The Church was suddenly in no position to order more cathedrals to be built.

Even if they had done so, they might not have been Gothic ones. The third and final blow to Freemasonry's standing was that the Gothic style, so dominant since the 1100s, was being supplanted by a return to the simpler classicist values of Roman architecture. Suddenly Masons were running short of work. They would never again recover their position as the most elevated and valued manual workers in the land.

From Operative to Speculative

The Masons' financial fortunes might have declined during the Renaissance period but the Craft still maintained an enviable social status. The covert fraternity was admired both for its architectural and geometric knowledge and its lofty aims of self-improvement, and as the sixteenth century neared its close there was a tendency for Masonic lodges to admit non-stonemasons – who tended mainly to be sympathetic aristocrats – as honorary members.

This trend began in Scotland, where Freemasonry had long been firmly established: indeed, the world's oldest surviving Masonic lodge, Kilwinning Lodge No 0, was formed there in 1140. At the end of the 1500s it was even rumoured that King James VI of Scotland had become an honorary Mason. Clearly, membership was no longer restricted to architects and stonecutters.

This was the crucial period in history when Freemasonry underwent a sea change from an elevated series of trade union guilds to a philosophical and moral fraternity open – in theory, at least – to all who wanted to join. This process was largely put on hold in the first part of the seventeenth century, as the English Civil Wars rent the country asunder, but as the Age of Reason dawned in the 1640s and 1650s, Freemasonry truly came into its own.

No longer willing to accept religious doctrine and dogma unquestioningly, people were now investing far more importance in scientific and cerebral analysis of the mysteries of everyday

* * * * * * * *

The Schaw Statutes

In 1598, William Schaw, the Master of Works for Scottish
ruler (and suspected Mason) King James VI, passed
two statutes seeking clearly to define the nature of
Freemasonry. The decrees stated the responsibilities and
duties of lodge members and set out the punishments
for unsatisfactory work and employing non-initiated
Masons. They also required all lodges to keep minutes
of every meeting, and obliged them to submit their
members to tests of their knowledge of Masonic history
and law.

* * * * * * * *

life. These progressive thinkers were greatly impressed with Freemasonry's stringent moral code
and search for self-betterment: to use Masonry's
language, the way that members sought to turn
themselves into beings as sturdy, worthy and
inspiring as a cathedral.

The traditional *operative* Freemasons who
worked daily with stone and gauge were thus
joined in the lodges by a new wave of *speculative*

Masons who had never wielded a chisel in their life. Some traditionalist members opposed the move, afraid that these newcomers would see no reason to keep their zealously guarded trade secrets. A few lodges even burned all written records. Yet before long such *accepted* or *admitted* Masons were accepted within the fraternity by all but the most reactionary stonecutters.

Freemasonry thus proudly took its place in the vanguard of progressive thought, alongside institutions such as the recently-formed Royal Society of London, a scientific thinking-shop: many illustrious figures such as Sir Christopher Wren and Elias Ashmole joined both organizations. Yet even amongst the hard intellectual rigour of the age, it is easy to believe such elevated men of reason must have enjoyed a private, boyish frisson at the arcane rituals and elaborate secrecy required to become a speculative Mason.

Dan Brown could be forgiven for latching eagerly onto the speculative Freemasons of the mid-seventeenth century as a plot device. Here, after all, was a covert conglomeration of the age's greatest and most renowned free thinkers, operating within a ritualistic secret society – who knows what perfidious plots they could have been hatching?

However, such speculation appears largely misplaced. There is no evidence that the Free-masons' lodges of this era were bent upon anything more than speculative contemplation of a fast-changing world, combined with a rigorous moral code. Members at this time still professed allegiance to God rather than a nebulous Supreme Being: their sole 'crime' in reactionary eyes was also to embrace the new-fangled Renaissance cult of rationalism.

Operative Masons' fortunes also received a spectacular boost in the middle of the century. The Great Fire of London of 1666 razed 40,000 dwellings to the ground and close to 100 churches in the capital. As architects and builders flocked to London, the number of Masons' lodges in the city rocketed accordingly. Yet this proved a short-lived gain, and by the start of the eighteenth century there were a mere six Masonic lodges in London. Other lodges were scattered across the country in an *ad hoc*, disjointed manner, and even within these fraternal chapters, observation of Masonic rituals and symbolism was declining.

Freemasonry clearly needed to organize or it would die.

The Grand Lodges

By the early eighteenth century, Freemasonry had become so informal that most lodges met only sporadically, at a public house convenient for its members. The four most significant lodges in London regularly convened at four separate alehouses: the Goose & Gridiron, next to the recently-completed St Paul's Cathedral; the Crown, in Parkers Lane near to Drury Lane; the Apple Tree tavern, in Charles Street on the fringes of Covent Garden's fruit market; and the Rummer & Grapes, close by the Palace of Westminster. None of these hostelries survive today.

In February 1717, senior figures from these four lodges gathered at the Apple Tree tavern for crisis talks. Sensing that Freemasonry was at a crossroads, these elders decided to put in place a coherent structure that would unify the entire movement. They also resolved to reintroduce

* * * * * * * *

Deference Within Masonry?

Despite Masonry's claims to eschewing social snobbery and prejudice, it is notable that no working stonemason has ever been voted Grand Master of the Grand Lodge of England. From 1717–21 only, the position was held by gentlemen, or speculative, Masons. Thereafter, the Grand Lodge has invariably voted aristocracy or, in recent years, royalty into its top post. The first Royal Family member to be Grand Master was King George III's brother, the Duke of Cumberland, in 1782. The current incumbent, HRH the Duke of Kent, was appointed in 1967.

* * * * * * * *

respect for the rituals and traditions that had made the fraternity unique and revered. So it was that, on 24 June 1717, London's senior Masons gathered at the Goose & Gridiron in the court-yard of St Paul's Cathedral, whose construction had been overseen by one of their number, Sir Christopher Wren, to form the Grand Lodge of England. As their first ever Grand Master they elected a speculative or *admitted* Mason, Anthony Sayer from the lodge at the Crown.

The founding of the Grand Lodge of England succeeded in giving Masonry the greater cohesion it required, but paradoxically it also caused rifts within the fraternity. Long-established lodges in Scotland and the north of England did not respond favourably to the Grand Lodge's unilateral declaration that it alone could recognize, or *charter*, new lodges, and that it was henceforth in regulatory charge of all existing lodges.

In 1725, northern lodges formed a rival Grand Lodge of All England at York – a body that lasted until 1790. Scotland, ever resentful of English rule, had no truck with London and formed its own completely independent Grand Lodge of St John of Scotland in 1736. Ireland, however, fell into line with the English Grand Lodge and formed its own Grand Lodge of Ireland under a charter from London.

* * * * * * * *

Antients and Moderns

In 1751 a Master Mason named Laurence Dermott, an Irishman living in London, formed a rival to the Grand Lodge of England called the Antient Grand Lodge. This group objected to the perceived progressive tendencies of the Grand Lodge of England, which it believed had degenerated into a mere philosophical talking-shop that was neglecting the essential rituals and traditions of Masonry. The Antients versus the Moderns dispute simmered within Freemasonry until 1813, when it was resolved by the creation of the United Grand Lodge of England (see page 53).

* * * * * * * *

Masonry gets a Constitutional

As part of its drive to reunite and redefine Freemasonry, in 1721 the Grand Lodge of England decided to create a Masonic constitution. It asked one Dr James Anderson, a Scottish nationalist and preacher living in London, to examine old Masonic documents and update them into one instructional manual to be distributed to all lodges as a definitive text.

The result, *The Constitution, History, Laws, Charges, Orders, Regulations and Usages of the Right Worshipful Fraternity of Accepted Free Masons, collected from their General Records and their Faithful Traditions of Many Ages*, was published in 1723. Also known as the Ancient Charges, or the Book of Constitutions, Anderson's script remains Freemasonry's most significant document, and is still read aloud annually in many Masonic lodges around the globe.

Taking its cue from the Regius Manuscript, the Book of Constitutions opens by making out-landish claims about the provenance of Masonry, claiming that not only was Adam the original architect and Noah a Mason, but Moses was a Grand Master! Yet it was the main body of the regulations, headed The Charges of a Free Mason, which was to drop a theological bombshell – and shape Freemasonry for centuries to come.

Until now, Masonry had routinely genuflected before God, with Christian prayers said in lodge meetings and references to the Holy Trinity scattered throughout some rituals. Anderson's

Constitutions abolished such devotions in favour of a nebulous, non-specific deism in the following paragraph:

A Mason is oblig'd by his Tenure, to obey the moral law: and if he rightly understands the Art, he will never be a stupid ATHEIST, nor an irreligious LIBERTINE. But though in ancient Times Masons were charged in every Country to be of the Religion of that Country or Nation, whatever it was, yet it is now thought more expedient only to oblige them to that Religion in which all Men agree, leaving their particular Opinions to themselves; that is, to be good Men and true, or men of Honour and Honesty, by whatever Denominations or Persuasions they may be distinguish'd ...

Henceforth, Freemasons would require new Entered Apprentices to pledge their belief in a Greater Being: without such faith, they believed initiates would be unable to undertake the journey of spiritual growth mapped out by the fraternity. But in the new spirit of non-sectarianism, this Supreme Being would take a new name: the Grand Architect of the Universe.

Aside from this radical departure, Anderson's

Constitutions were largely a summation of existing Masonic law. As per the Regius Manuscript, Masons were ordered to be 'a peaceable subject to the Civil Powers' and never to plot against king or country. The Charges also emphasized that Freemasonry is inherently democratic: 'No Master or Warden is chosen by Seniority, but by his Merit'.

Another key Charge stressed the importance of courtesy and consideration amongst Freemasons, and – after a clause warning against excess intake of alcohol – Anderson added a few lines intended to maintain this internal harmony:

'Therefore no private Piques or Quarrels must be brought within the Door of the Lodge, far less any Quarrels about Religion, or Nations, or State Policy, we being only, as Masons of the Catholick Religion above-mentioned; we are also of all Nations, Tongues, Kindreds and Languages, and are resolved against all Politicks, as what never yet conduc'd to the Welfare of the Lodge, nor ever will.'

These words established the crucial Masonic tenet that religion and politics should never be discussed with the walls of a lodge. It is a stipulation that can be regarded as hugely ironic: the secretive organization that many detractors believe to be a seething mass of dissent and subversion actively legislating against discussing the state of the world.

After the establishment of the Grand Lodge of England and the drafting of the Constitutions, Masonry underwent a period of expansion in England and elsewhere. By 1730, over 100 lodges had pledged allegiance to the Grand Lodge, and 1737 saw the first (publicly admitted, at least) Royal Freemason: Frederick Lewis the Prince of Wales, the son of King George II.

As the British Empire expanded throughout the eighteenth century, Freemasonry made similar territorial quantum leaps. By the end of the century, lodges had been established in Spain, India, South America and even parts of Southeast Asia. As we shall shortly see, however, by far the most significant - indeed, revolutionary - events in international Masonic history were set to play out in the United States and France.

Rome is not amused

The 1700s was not an era of unbridled growth and prosperity for Masonry. The Catholic Church, fighting Protestantism's rampant encroachment onto its turf right across Europe, was less than enamoured of Freemasonry's exclusive and secretive reputation, and Rome's disapproval turned to outright horror when Anderson's Book of Constitutions dispensed with the Holy Trinity within the lodge walls.

In 1738, Pope Clement XII issued a papal bull threatening any Catholics who were also Freemasons with excommunication. The following year, he upped the ante with a second decree that all Catholics within the Papal States (Italy, plus parts of France) who were found to be Masons would be executed.

Some Freemasons found themselves at the wrong end of the Inquisition in Spain, Italy and Portugal, and in 1884 Pope Leo XII came close to calling the fraternity satanic in his notorious *encyclical Humanum Genus* edict. Like many popes after him, he was horrified not only by Masonry's perceived deism but also by its refusal to allow

* * * * * * * *

Catholicism vs Freemasonry Today

Freemasons hoped that the Roman Catholic Church's position on Masonry had softened towards the end of the twentieth century. The Church's 1917 Code of Canon Law had declared Masonic membership punishable by automatic excommunication, but when this major doctrinal document was revised in 1983, Freemasonry had vanished from the list of prohibited 'secret societies'. However, later in the same year the current Pope Benedict XVI, who was then a senior Church functionary, made it known that Masons remain 'in a state of grave sin' and are barred from taking communion. There appears little prospect of change as long as Benedict XVI is in charge at the Vatican.

* * * * * * * *

members to even speak of religion during Masonic meetings.

The Antients vs Moderns schism that had ripped Masonry asunder for sixty years was resolved in 1813, when the two factions joined forces to form the United Grand Lodge of England (UGLE). This new body thus became the main legislative and administrative authority for English Masonry, but declined to impose standardized wording on all rituals and ceremonies, instead leaving individual lodges scope to shape their own vows.

The UGLE agreement, however, included a classic fudge caused by a major divergence in Masonic thinking across the world. The Modern school, represented by the original Grand Lodge of England, felt that the established three degrees of Masonry – Entered Apprentice, Fellow of the Craft and Master Mason – were all that were needed. The Antients held the opinion that another piece was required to complete the puzzle.

Feeling that the Master Mason degree as it stood did not complete the tale it purported to tell (namely, the murder of Hiram Abiff – *see* Chapter 3: Inside The Lodge: Masonic Rituals and Symbols), the Antients conceived an additional degree, the Holy Royal Arch – indeed, there is categorical evidence that at very early Masonic meetings, this ceremony formed part of the basic Master Mason degree. Loath to tamper with the long-established three degrees but keen to get the Antients on board, the UGLE resolved the dispute by means of a carefully worded compromise:

> 'Pure Ancient Masonry is to consist of three degrees, and no more; viz, those of the Entered Apprentice, the Fellowcraft, and the Master Mason including the Supreme Order of the Holy Royal Arch.'

This deliberately convoluted phrasing opened the way for UGLE-affiliated English lodges to practise the York Rite, should they be so minded (see page 199). Along with the Scottish Rite, this series of elaborate rituals allows Freemasons to collect appendant degrees after they have qualified as a Master Mason (see Chapter 3).

The formation of UGLE became known as the Reformation of Freemasonry and effectively settled all squabbles within the English Masonic fraternity, paving the way for an unprecedented period of stability and growth within the movement. However, circumstances were far more volatile in two other key Masonic territories – France and America.

Freemasonry in France

Freemasonry as it is practised in England, America and English-speaking territories around the globe is known as Anglo Masonry. The second largest strain, Continental Masonry, originated in France and also dominates in most European territories and across Central and South America.

Freemasonry arrived in France after King James II of England (who was also King James VI of Scotland) was dethroned in 1688 for attempting to return now-Protestant Britain to Catholicism. James fled to France followed by many thousands of courtiers and disciples who wanted to return the usurped king to power – these acolytes became known as the Jacobites.

There were many Freemasons, both English and Scottish, amongst the Jacobites' number, and after copious lodges appeared across the country, a Grand Lodge was formed in Paris in 1728. Numerous competing Grand Lodges quickly sprang up including 1733's Grand Orient de France, a body whose maverick tendencies would later cause shock waves.

The Antients vs Moderns squabble also spread

across the Channel, but the French version had a far more poetic and romantic aspect. In 1737, a Scottish Mason in Paris called Andrew Michael Ramsay published a pamphlet that argued that Freemasonry was directly descended from the Knights Templar, the legendary order of Christian warrior knights active in the Holy Lands in the twelfth and thirteenth centuries (see Chapter 2: The Notional History of Freemasonry: Great Conspiracy Theories). This singular theory requires a convoluted reading of highly circumstantial evidence plus a determined suspension of critical disbelief (and has thus provided the bedrock for Dan Brown's ludicrous but lucrative fiction-writing career to date).

After publicizing his theorem, sometimes known as the Ramsay Oration, the quixotic Ramsay disappeared from public view. Nevertheless, his ideas fired the fevered imaginations of French Freemasons, who began to introduce into their ceremonies ever more exotic degrees and rituals based upon biblical ideas and the Knights Templar myth. Eventually, US Masonic scholar Albert Pike formalized these innovations into the Scottish Rite in 1859.

Freemasonry expanded rapidly in France until the 1789 French Revolution, in which it was believed that many leading Masons were heavily involved. This appears hugely likely: Freemasonry by now lay in the forefront of French progressive and dissident thinking, and a telling clue is that the revolutionaries even co-opted French Masonry's motto of *'Libertie! Egalitie! Fraternitie!'* as their own rallying cry.

Nevertheless, as post-Revolution French society collapsed into anarchy as the revolutionaries turned on each other, the wider populace began the quest for scapegoats and found it convenient to lay much of the blame at the Masons' door. From being viewed as a chic and bohemian organization, French Freemasonry was suddenly forced to go deep underground.

Masonry's profile in France remained subterranean until the accession to power of Napoleon Bonaparte, a leader believed by many to have been a Mason (though this was never proved). During the nineteenth century the Grand Orient de France became the predominant Grand Lodge in this land of many Grand Lodges, but in the 1870s this idiosyncratic organization effectively

* * * * * * * *

Dr Joseph Guillotine

Conspiracy theorists wishing to substantiate their claim that the Masons have been a sinister and subversive influence on society since biblical times have made much of the Masons' undeniable involvement in the French Revolution. The Freemasons' claims of innocence are not helped by the fact that Dr Guillotine, the inventor of the machine that decapitated thousands of French bourgeoisie in the Place de la Concord, was a Mason.

* * * * * * * *

ostracized itself from the main body of world Freemasonry.

Ever since the Anderson Constitutions of 1723, Freemasonry had required all new initiates to pledge devotion to its non-denominational Supreme Being, the Grand Architect of the Universe. In 1877, the Grand Orient de France dispensed with this requirement and began to admit not only the non-believers that Anderson had dismissed as 'stupid atheists' but also women.

This typically radical manoeuvre met with a horrified reaction from Grand Lodges around the globe, who immediately 'derecognized' the Grand Orient. Even to this day, the Orient remains un-recognized by the majority of worldwide Grand Lodges, a situation about which, it must be said, it appears heroically unconcerned.

Today, Freemasonry in France is less structured and coherent than in any other nation. There are approximately 120,000 Masons in France who are affiliated to no less than fifteen Grand Lodges of which the 'official' recognized authority, the Grande Loge Nationale Francaise, is by no means the most powerful or even the largest.

Instead, with at least one thousand affiliated lodges and more than 40,000 paid-up mem-bers, the 'stupid atheist'-welcoming, women-embracing Grand Orient de France remains by far the most populous Masonic body in France despite the vigorous disapproval of the entire world of Anglo Masonry. Is there a Masonic term for *Vive la difference?*

* * * * * * * *

Recognition

Grand Lodges around the world are said to 'recognize' other Grand Lodges who obey the basic precepts of Masonry (broadly, they must be originally descended by some means from the first Grand Lodges of England, Scotland or Ireland, must declare faith in the Grand Architect of the Universe and must not admit women). Freemasons are allowed to visit any lodge that obeys these strictures, but are forbidden to cross the threshold of any unrecognized body. Despite this, many rogue or irregular organizations exist entirely happily outside of the international Masonic mainstream.

* * * * * * * *

Freemasonry in America

Freemasonry in France began with an influx of Masons from England before veering off in an idiosyncratic and individualistic direction. Freemasonry in America did the same, but with one major difference – Masons were present at the birth of this great nation and played a limited but significant role in shaping its character and ethos.

The first Freemasons to set sail for America did so shortly after the forming of the original Grand Lodge of England in 1717. The Grand Lodge set up colonial offices to charter lodges and the first 'official' US charter was granted in 1733 to St John's Grand Lodge, Boston, who met at a local tavern called the Green Dragon. By then, however, independent, non-recognized lodges had also appeared across New England.

America became a battleground for competing British Grand Lodges. In 1752, the Grand Lodge of Scotland chartered a lodge – St Andrew's Lodge No 82 – in Boston, causing outrage at St John's Grand Lodge, who felt they alone could charter lodges in Massachusetts. The grievance was exacerbated when St Andrew's began to confer a new Masonic degree honouring the Knights Templar that was not sanctioned by the Grand Lodge of England.

These squabbles were made to look pro-foundly parochial, however, by what was to follow. American resentment at taxes levied by London was running high, and on 16 December 1773, a gang of men heavily disguised as Native

* * * * * * * *

Prince Hall Masons

Born in Barbados in 1748, Prince Hall is believed to have been the first black Freemason. He and fourteen other black men were initiated into an Irish military lodge in Boston in 1775. When the regiment and lodge moved on, Prince Hall was given permission to form the so-called African Lodge, which had only limited rights: they were not allowed, for example, to initiate new members. After the War of Independence ended, Grand Master Prince Hall applied for African Lodge to join the Grand Lodge of Massachusetts but was turned down on – there is little doubt – racist grounds. Undeterred, Hall secured a charter from the Grand Lodge of England before, in 1827, African Lodge broke all links with England and elevated itself to a Grand Lodge. Freemasonry – like society, far more enlightened today – is now determinedly multi-racial, but worldwide around 250,000 Masons belong to one of 5,000 largely black Prince Hall-affiliated lodges.

* * * * * * * *

Americans boarded three British merchant ships at Boston Harbour and hurled over 300 crates of tea into the sea. Many eyewitnesses claimed the Tea Party protesters had made their way to the quayside from the Green Dragon ... the home of St John's Grand Lodge.

The role of Freemasonry in the American War of Independence of 1775–83 is hotly disputed, and we will examine this contentious topic closely in the next chapter, The Notional History of Freemasonry: Great Conspiracy Theories. However, there are certain facts that indisputably link the fraternity to the American Revolution.

Many Freemasons were war heroes. Two of the people who drafted the 1776 Declaration of Independence, Benjamin Franklin and Robert Livingston, are among the most illustrious figures in US Masonic history, and at least nine, and possibly fifteen, of the document's signatories were Masons. Eleven years later, one-third of the thirty-nine people who put their names to the US Constitution were members of the Craft.

It's clear, then, that many of America's Founding Fathers were steeped in the philosophy and lore of the Freemasons, who were, after all, one of the land's most fashionable and intellectual social societies of the time. Yet it is notable that no serious historians of this era have claimed that subversive tendrils, buried deep in the nation's marrow in the 1700s, continue to shape US society today.

The most famous Freemason in history – George Washington – was inaugurated as the first President of the United States in 1789. A Master Mason since 1753, Washington never neglected the fraternity even after he ascended to the highest office. In 1793, he marched in his Masonic apron, along with fellow Masons, to lay the cornerstone for the construction of the Capitol building in Washington DC.

Freemasonry underwent spectacular growth in the US in the early 1800s as polite society realized its currency among the Founding Fathers. By mid-century, virtually every state in the union had formed a Grand Lodge. The York and Scottish rites also rocketed in popularity as lodges from New York to New Mexico warmed to the showy and dramatic ceremonials of these appendant degrees (see Chapter 3: Inside The Lodge: Masonic Rituals and Symbols).

*   *   *   *   *   *   *   *

Swearing on a Masonic Bible

When George Washington was sworn in as US President in New York on 30 April 1789, he took the oath on a Bible supplied by the city's St John's Lodge No 1. That same Bible has been used for the inauguration of five further American presidents, including Dwight D. Eisenhower (1953), Jimmy Carter (1977) and George H.W. Bush (1990). President George W. Bush also asked to use the St John's Lodge Bible for his inauguration in 2001 but was unable to do so as torrential rain on the day would have damaged the by-now highly fragile book.

*   *   *   *   *   *   *   *

The movement, however, was not without detractors. Numerous citizens and local leaders worried over what could be unfolding behind the guarded doors of the Masonic lodges that were appearing across the country, and senior Church figures were agitated about Masonry's ejection of the Christian God from its rituals. Then a bizarre event in upstate New York gave ammunition to these critics and sent the Freemasonry movement reeling.

Masons – or murderers?

In a tiny upstate New York town named Batavia in 1826, a disillusioned Mason named William Morgan declared that he would write a book exposing every secret sign, grip and ritual of Masonry. A gang of local Masons immediately kidnapped Morgan, who was never seen again. His abductors claimed they had paid him to emigrate to Canada, but his friends alleged he had been subjected to a Masonic 'ritual killing' before his body was hurled into Lake Ontario.

After a trial which saw six defendants evade murder charges and receive only token sentences, the controversy escalated after it emerged that the trial judge, prosecutor and most jurors were Freemasons – as was the town's Governor, one Dewitt Clinton. The Morgan scandal enflamed local anti-Masonic sentiment and soon grew into a national *cause celebre*.

In 1828, upstate New York hosted an anti-

Masons conference. Three years later the anti-Masonic Party scored nearly 10 per cent of the vote in a Presidential election, including taking the state in Vermont. Congress passed vehement anti-Masonic legislation. At the time of Morgan's disappearance, there were over 100,000 Masons across America. By 1837 only one-third were still members. Over a century before McCarthy, Free-masonry had become an un-American activity.

Masonry reacted to this ostracism from US society by embracing a new sobriety – quite literally. Alcohol, previously a crucial element of Masonic dinners, was banned from all lodge buildings. Rituals and ceremonies usurped socializing as Freemasonry embraced a new purity of purpose: the amount of money given to charitable causes was also ratcheted up.

After the American Civil War of 1861–65, Masonry Stateside regained its footing. Member-ship once again rose steadily, largely through the popular appeal of the theatrical dramatics of the Scottish Rite, whose concocted tales of biblical fables and Knights Templar were comprehensively rewritten by obsessive Masonic scholar Albert Pike.

* * * * * * * *

American Civil War

Despite the slump in membership caused by the Morgan scandal, there were still nearly forty Grand Lodges in America at the onset of the Civil War, and inevitably Masons from different parts of the country found themselves in mortal combat with fellow Masons – some of whom wore Masonic insignia and badges on their uniforms in the hope of eliciting mercy from fellow brothers in the event of capture. Almost 18,000 Freemasons fought at the Battle of Gettysburg in 1863, and nearly one-third of them lost their lives.

* * * * * * * *

Masonry's rehabilitation in the US was completed in the early years of the twentieth century, when lodges across America became hugely involved in public good works, financing the building of many orphanages and old people's homes and providing scholarship funds for students from disadvantaged backgrounds. This proved a tremendous public relations fillip, and by the close of the 1920s there were over three million Freemasons in America.

* * * * * * * *

The Very First Time I Saw Your Fez

The largest Masonic charitable donations in the US come from the Shriners, the most bizarre and high-profile of all Freemason organizations. Formed in New York in 1879 as a reaction to the post-Morgan Masons' newfound puritanism, the Ancient Arabic Nobles of the Mystic Shrine are the zany wing of the Masonic movement. Dedicated to outrageous socializing and charitable fund-raising, the Shriners have built, and continue to finance, a string of children's hospitals across the States. Best known for their self-consciously wacky parades featuring them driving miniature cars and wearing fezzes, they are not without controversy: many Muslims resent the Shriners' facetious appropriation of Arabic names and culture in their rituals.

* * * * * * * *

Freemasonry and the Second World War

The Second World War had a profound effect on Freemasonry. Like many of history's dictators, Adolf Hitler abhorred Masons, feeling them to be 'servants of the Jew' and regularly accusing them of treason. Many Masons were sent to concentration camps while, in Italy, President Benito Mussolini also banned Masonry.

Naturally, Masons in occupied territories suffered the most, with Masons in France, Italy and Spain being obsessively persecuted. When the Nazis invaded Czechoslovakia they arrested 4,000 Masons, sending many of them to concentration camps. Remarkably, in 1942 Hitler even declared Freemasons and 'the ideological enemies of national socialism who are allied with them' to be 'the originators of this war' – which could safely be said to be news to Grand Masters across the globe, who struggled to recall exactly when their lodges had invaded Poland. Nevertheless, the European leader who stood firm against the Third Reich was a renowned Freemason – British Prime Minister, Sir Winston Churchill.

Post-war to the Twenty-first Century

The 1950s was a golden age for modern Freemasonry, with fraternities of every hue in vogue in the States and Masonic membership swelling, in part due to the heroic status of leading Masons like Presidents Franklin D. Roosevelt and Harry S. Truman. By 1959, there were nearly five million Masons in America – a figure that is unlikely ever to be surpassed.

Unsurprisingly, the following decade was more barren for the movement as the generation of free love, Woodstock and anti-Vietnam protests looked askance at a seemingly dated and furtive organization of arcane rituals, secret passwords and funny handshakes. Ironically, this fraternity that had been so often condemned by Church and State throughout history was now viewed as part of the fusty Establishment.

Freemasonry's image in Britain was dented in the 1970s by a handful of high-profile corruption scandals involving senior police, local authority members and even criminals, but the millennium ended with the fraternity on a plateau of around five million Masons worldwide and the American

Masonic movement launching a major, high-profile recruitment drive.

From medieval stonemasons' guilds to the twenty-first century, via the French Revolution, the Boston Tea Party and Nazi persecution, the history of Freemasonry is a picaresque marvel in its own right. With a cast list taking in Hiram Abiff, King Athelstan, George Washington and Sir Winston Churchill, the most gifted writers of fiction would find it difficult to render the story of the Craft any more fantastical or extraordinary.

This does not mean that they haven't tried. With *The Solomon Key*, Dan Brown is only the latest in a parade of alternative historians and novelists who have cherry-picked choice moments from Biblical legends, ancient myths, conspiracy theories and historical coincidences to imply that something is very rotten in the state of Freemasonry.

Brown certainly stitches together his fantastical plot devices skilfully and it would be overly churlish to diminish the pleasure gained by his vast worldwide readership from his labyrinthine detective fantasies. However, in the interests of accuracy and a real-life assessment of the historical import and lineage of the Freemasons, it is the duty of this book to point out that the vast majority of *The Solomon Key*'s clues simply don't add up …

2

THE NOTIONAL HISTORY
OF FREEMASONRY:
GREAT CONSPIRACY
THEORIES

It is impossible to deny that it is largely Freemasonry's own fault that so many fantastical theories circulate about the movement's origins. With its romanticized ceremonies and a constitution that claims lineage from Moses and King Solomon's Temple, the fraternity can hardly complain when the likes of Dan Brown pull a few sleight-of-hand tricks to weave dramatic fiction from their history for their own purposes.

Brown was not the first, and nor will he be the last. Ever since the Age of Enlightenment, when the invention of the printing press sent suspicious outsiders running to write lurid exposés of the 'un-Godly' Masons, the movement has had to face countless accusations of ulterior motives and nefarious activities carried out within its walls.

Anti-Masonic allegations come in all shapes and sizes, from the deliriously imaginative romantics who perceive the brotherhood as being in secret possession of the Holy Grail seized from King Solomon's Temple by the Knights Templar, to protesters who sense the hand of a lodge behind controversial local planning or business decisions. The worldwide web reveals there are also still plenty of malcontents who are convinced that Freemasonry exerts invisible control over the world banking system en route to establishing its own sinister New World Order.

Dan Brown chooses to pursue the engaging theory that America's Founding Fathers envisaged the US as the ultimate example of Masonry's utopianism in action. The author claims that these shaping figures hid a Masonic symbol in the Great Seal of the nation, and even laid out the streets of Washington DC in a way that reflected Masonic tenets.

Underlying this plot device is the major assumption that Brown made in *The Da Vinci Code*, with which Masonic teaching is also in full cahoots: that Freemasonry possesses a lurid hidden history that reaches back a full two millennia before the forming of the medieval stonemasons' guilds. We should begin this consideration of anti-Masonic conspiracy theories by examining this hypothetical parallel history of Freemasonry.

THE NOTIONAL HISTORY OF FREEMASONRY

The Regius Manuscript and James Anderson's 1723 Book of Constitutions, as we have learned, both laid claim to Masonry possessing Biblical origins: Anderson even went right back to the source and claimed that the first man alive, Adam, was an architect and therefore a Mason. It's hugely telling that Masonry's first chroniclers sought to give the movement a history as deep-rooted as mankind itself.

The Wisdom of Solomon

King Solomon remains regarded as the theoretical inaugural Most Excellent Grand Master of Freemasonry, and Masonic lore holds that there is a direct lineage from this legendary monarch to Freemasonry today. The first link in this chain is said to be an ancient mystical collective of architects known as the Fraternity of Dionysian Artificers.

The Dionysian Artificers were supposedly sent by Hiram, King of Tyre to aid King Solomon in the building of his temple on Mount Moriah. They had already built gleaming temples across the Middle East and would have been a welcome addition to the workforce – the mysterious, doomed Hiram Abiff may even have been their leader, a pre-Freemasonry equivalent to a Masonic Grand Master.

The parallel history of Freemasonry claims that after King Solomon's Temple was completed, the Dionysian Artificers taught new initiates a discipline that combined architectural know-how with the wisdom and morality of Solomon. Over the following centuries they bestowed this

* * * * * * * *

Dionysian Artificers

The Fraternity of the Dionysian Artificers of Tyre are said to have been a Tyrian and Phoenician sect of builders who pre-dated the Masons but shared many characteristics. Masonic historian Manly Hall says they 'constituted an ancient secret society, its principles and doctrines much like the modern Freemasonic order … they possessed a secret language and a system of marking their stones.' He also claims they called themselves the 'Sons of Solomon' and taught a moral code based on the tools of the building trade.

* * * * * * * *

practical and spiritual education on new initiates before eventually passing it on to Pythagoras, who had moved from Greece to Italy in the sixth century BC to form a school of religion and mathematics.

This knowledge supposedly passed from Pythagorean teaching into the architectural colleges, or *collegia*, formed by the Romans between the second century BC and the fourth century AD.

These Roman Colleges of Architects were led by a master and two wardens, and the remains of a school at Pompeii confirms they seem to have used drawings of architectural tools as part of a practical *and* symbolic education in the same manner as the Dionysian Artificers.

After the fall of the Roman Empire in the fifth century AD, the barbarians reduced the *collegia* to rubble. However, a handful of architects from the Roman Colleges supposedly took refuge on an island on Lake Como in Lombardy, northern Italy. These hardy few, who became known as the Comacine Masons or Comacine Masters, preserved the teachings of the Dionysian Artificers and Pythagoras during the Dark Ages.

The notional history of Masonry claims that the Comacine Masons formed guilds named *loggia* or lodges, developed secret handshakes and passwords and wore white aprons at their meetings. They continued to make use of building-related allegorical symbols, including King Solomon's knot, the Arch, an architect's square and an infinite intertwined length of cord.

The most hardcore Masonic historians claim these *Magistri Comacini* were even hoarding trade

* * * * * * * *

Four Crowned Martyrs

A possibly apocryphal story tells of the Roman Emperor Diocletian, who ruled 284–305 AD, ordering four Christian students at one of the Roman *collegia* to make a statue of the Roman god Aesculapius. These students refused to betray their faith and were duly executed. This tale of the Four Crowned Martyrs is retold in the Regius Manuscript (1390), one of the most important documents in Masonic history.

* * * * * * * *

secrets used by Noah to build his ark. The final link in the notional history chain occurred when a few Comacine Masons went to England in the tenth or eleventh century and shared their covert knowledge with English stonemasons who, suitably inspired, began to construct Gothic cathedrals. The far-fetched conclusion? Freemasonry is derived directly from the wisdom and teachings of King Solomon!

This seductive argument has only one fundamental flaw – that it is absolute gale-force gibberish. Biographers of Pythagoras make no mention of the great mathematician encountering any rogue members of the Fraternity of Dionysian Architects, nor of schooling his students in the architectural niceties of Noah's Ark. Likewise, the Comacine Masons were a minor sect whose importance is greatly overstated by this convenient, but convoluted, Masonic rewriting of history, and there is no evidence beyond supposition that any of them travelled to Britain.

It is a plot device worthy of the most masterful authors of historical fiction, but the fantasy of an unbroken spiritual *and* physical lineage from King Solomon remains Freemasonry's equivalent of an Old Testament fable.

FREEMASONRY: GREAT CONSPIRACY THEORIES

1) THE KNIGHTS TEMPLAR CONNECTION

The *Magistri Comanici*-dependent alternative history of Freemasonry can, perhaps, be regarded as an essentially benign and harmless fairy tale with a highly tenuous relationship with reality (a categorization that arguably applies equally well to Dan Brown's detective fiction). However, both Brown and more serious scholars give far more weight to a rival theory of Masonry's heritage – that the movement is directly descended from both the Holy Lands and King Solomon's Temple via the intervention of the Knights Templar.

Who were the Knights Templar?

In the eleventh century, relations between the Islamic rulers of Jerusalem and the Christians of western Europe grew uneasy. There were numerous reports of Christian pilgrims to the Holy Lands being attacked and robbed by Muslims, and in 1096 Pope Urban II called for the armies of Catholic Europe to rise up and retake the sacred city of Jerusalem from the 'occupying infidels'.

The result was the Crusades of 1096–1250, still the most notorious and resented period in Islamic history. Over the decades, seven separate armies of 'Crusader' knights, clad in white robes bearing red crosses, marched on Jerusalem, routing the Islamic caliphate and returning Jerusalem to Catholic control.

Unsurprisingly, this medieval take on military shock-and-awe tactics led to even more attacks on individual Christian pilgrims by the disgruntled Muslim residents of the Holy Lands, and in 1118 a Burgundy knight, Hugues de Payens (also known as Yves de Faillon) formed an order of warrior monks to escort bands of pilgrims to Jerusalem and ensure their safety. This army of men was initially known as the Poor Knights of Christ.

The knights set up a base on Mount Moriah, with scant regard for Islamic sensibilities, inside the sacred al-Aqsa mosque on the site of the former King Solomon's Temple. With this act of appropriation, they changed the name of their order to the Poor Knights of Christ and the Temple of Solomon – or, as they are universally known, the Knights Templar.

Despite pledges of poverty and piety, the Knights Templars' wealth quickly grew. Adopted as Holy Warriors by the Catholic Church at the

Council of Troyes in 1128, they were permitted to keep all money and possessions they looted from Muslims. The Knights owned vast tracts of land across Syria and Palestine until Islamic forces regained control of Jerusalem in 1239.

Evicted from the Middle East, the Knights Templar settled in Cyprus and France and became international bankers. Their leader (or Grand Master) at the end of the thirteenth century was Jacques de Molay, a French monk whose piety stood in stark contrast to the venality of many of his knights. However, in 1307 the Knights Templars' Catholic sponsors turned on the order.

Aided by Pope Clement V, King Philip IV of France – who was jealous of the Knights' vast wealth – arrested all Knights Templars in France and seized their holdings. Pope Clement V ordered all the remaining European Catholic nations to do the same. Jacques de Molay and other senior Templars were imprisoned, tortured and charged with heresy.

The allegations levelled against the Knights Templar were spectacular and varied – that they had mocked Christ, spat on the Holy Cross, indulged in homosexual orgies and worshipped a pagan idol named Baphomet (see page 115). Jacques de Molay and other Templars 'admitted' these charges under the duress of Inquisitors but later recanted the confessions, and in 1314 de Molay was burned at the stake on an island on the Seine outside Notre-Dame.

It is claimed that as de Molay endured the flames, he proclaimed the Knights Templars' innocence and predicted that King Philip IV and Pope Clement V would both die within the year – a prophesy that came true. In a remarkable twist to this tale, in 2001 a Vatican archivist unearthed a document that revealed that Pope Clement V had declared the Knights Templar to be innocent of all charges and pardoned the order shortly before he died.

The Secrets of the Templars?

Far from being mere mercenary medieval warriors, the Knights Templar have come to be regarded in many eyes as exotic, near-mystical beings. They are said to have possessed secret, possibly sacred or even satanic knowledge. One early twentieth century Masonic scholar, CW Leadbeater, claimed that the Templars were privy to 'the Hidden Wisdom of Europe': venerable occultist Aleister Crowley was also fascinated by the order.

Dan Brown portrays the Knights Templar as conveyers of the 'Sangreal' documents, an element of his spurious Holy Grail, in both *The Da Vinci Code* and *The Solomon Key*. And the Scottish Rite of Freemasonry founded by Andrew Michael Ramsay in 1737 (see page 57) argues that the Knights Templar were the conduit by which King Solomon's wisdom was passed to modern Freemasonry.

These theories rest on the assumption that the Templars gained mystical knowledge or even physical treasure while billeted next to the remains of King Solomon's Temple on Mount Moriah. Their proponents believe it is possible they encountered secret fraternities founded two millennia earlier by the Dionysian Artificers of Tyre, whose members could have told them tales such as the murder of Hiram Abiff.

In *The Da Vinci Code*, Dan Brown has the Knights Templar spiriting 'four chests of documents ... that have been the object of count-less Grail quests throughout history' away from the Temple crypt. His source appears to be archaeological reports that the Templars were constantly excavating the Temple area while sojourned on the Mount.

In truth, these theories are profoundly un-feasible. It is highly unlikely that significant numbers of Dionysian Artificers of Tyre, having travelled from Phoenicia in 957 BC to begin work on King Solomon's Temple, would then settle in Jerusalem, and that their descendants, almost two millennia later, would share secret or sacred knowledge with the occupying forces of the Knights Templar.

By the same token, King Solomon's Temple had been razed to the ground twice and replaced by the al-Aqsa mosque by the time the Templars arrived in 1118 AD. The idea that the 'Sangreal documents' nestled undisturbed in the mosque's crypt for 2,000 years before falling into the laps of the Knights Templar beggars belief – and is one of the many suspect plot devices found within *The Da Vinci Code*.

* * * * * * * *

The Dead Sea Scrolls

One source for the belief that treasure was hidden beneath King Solomon's Temple is the Copper Scroll, one of the Dead Sea Scrolls discovered hidden in caves near Jerusalem between 1947–56. Written by the mystic Hebrew sect the Essenes around 200 BC, the Copper Scroll makes the claim that gold, silver, precious perfumes and documents were concealed under the Temple and throughout Israel. The Essenes may have shared certain behaviour patterns with Freemasonry – including a love of geometry and Pythagorean theorem.

* * * * * * * *

From Templars to Masons?

When King Philip IV and Pope Clement V declared war on the Templars in 1307, thousands of Knights were arrested in France and put to the sword. However, some historians believe that many others escaped the purge, possibly after a tip-off, and dispersed to Protestant-leaning countries where the Pope's word carried little weight.

In their 1989 Masonry-based novel *The Temple and the Lodge*, 'alternative historians' Richard Leigh and Michael Baigent describe troupes of escaping Knights Templar fleeing to Scotland. (Dan Brown is certainly enamoured of their work – *The Da Vinci Code* mentioned their 1982 novel, *Holy Blood, Holy Grail*, as well as jokingly conflating their names to make a fictional character, Leigh Teabing. Leigh and Baigent are somewhat less impressed with Brown – in late 2005 they issued a writ accusing him of plagiarism, though Brown was cleared of all charges).

Scotland would have made sense as a Templar destination. Papal bulls were meaningless there: King Robert the Bruce had been excommunicated by Rome in 1305 after murdering John Comyn, his rival for the Scottish throne. Scotland was also at war with England, and the King would have welcomed any military assistance from these famously ferocious monks.

To all intents and purposes, the Knights Templar vanished off the radar and ceased to exist after the purge of 1307. However, one strain of

* * * * * * * *

Were Templars at Bannockburn?

In 1314, King Robert the Bruce's army scored a heroic victory against the numerically superior forces of English King Edward II at Bannockburn by Stirling Castle. Reports of the battle suggest the English soldiers were on top until, after hours of fierce fighting, the Scottish ranks were swollen by the sudden appearance of a troop of skilled warriors – leading some Masonic historians to suggest that these men were Knights Templars, offering their services in gratitude to King Robert for offering them safe haven from Catholic persecution. No verifiable evidence exists to support this claim.

* * * * * * * *

Freemasonic history suggests that after some Templars arrived in Scotland, they lived a low-profile existence on islands off the west coast then moved to Aberdeen, where they joined forces with existing local stonemasons guilds and founded speculative Masonry.

Even by the fantastical standards of parallel

Masonic provenance, it is a historical and imaginative quantum leap to perceive Freemasonry as passing directly from French Catholic warrior monks on Mount Moriah to hewers of stone in northern Scotland. Yet there is one piece of evidence to support this extraordinary theorem – the existence of the chapel at Rosslyn.

The Mystery of Rosslyn Chapel

Built between 1440–80 and situated seven miles south of Edinburgh, Rosslyn Chapel was designed by Sir William Sinclair (or St Clair), a member of a noble Scottish family rumoured to have links with the Knights Templar (a direct descendant of Sinclair, also called William Sinclair, was to become the first Grand Master Mason of Scotland in 1602).

The chapel is covered with arcane symbols – some of which appear to refer to Freemasonry. The ornate Apprentice Pillar and Master Pillar could echo the twin Jachin and Boaz pillars of King Solomon's Temple, while a ceiling carving of a wounded man is said by Masonic scholars to show

* * * * * * * *

'Freemasonry, in the form we would recognise today, started at the building of Rosslyn Chapel near Edinburgh'

Dr Robert Lomas, Master Mason, lecturer at Bradford University and prolific Masonic author

* * * * * * * *

the murder of Hiram Abiff, the 'widow's son' of ancient lore.

Most remarkably, a carving on a window frame in the southwest corner of the chapel appears to depict Masonry's Entered Apprentice degree ritual. A blindfolded man kneels between two pillars with a Bible in one hand and a length of rope around his neck. Before him – holding the end of the rope – stands a man seemingly clad in the distinctive robe of a Knight Templar.

Masonic historians have hailed Rosslyn Chapel as the missing link between the Knights Templar and speculative Freemasonry. In their 1998 study *The Second Messiah: Templars, the Turin Shroud and the Great Secret of Freemasonry*, Christopher Knight and Robert Lomas argue that Rosslyn is a replica of King Solomon's Temple, and far more besides:

> *'Rosslyn was not a simple chapel: it was a post-Templar shrine built to house the scrolls found by Hugues de Payens and his team under the Holy of Holies of the last Temple at Jerusalem! Beneath our feet was the most priceless treasure in Christendom.'*

Ever the pseudo-historical magpie, Dan Brown appropriates this idea in *The Da Vinci Code*, where Robert Langdon declares the 'Sangreal documents' to be buried beneath a motif on the floor of Rosslyn Chapel that could – just about – be interpreted as a Seal of Solomon. In Masonic symbolism, the Seal is traditionally accompanied by the motto *Nil nisi clavis deest:* 'Only the key is wanting' (*see* Chapter 3: Inside The Lodge: Masonic Rituals and Symbols).

Today Rosslyn Chapel hosts Scottish Rite-based Masonic ceremonies and is visited by Freemasons from across the globe. Tom Hanks and Audrey Tatou filmed *The Da Vinci Code* scenes there, and the reliably opportunistic Dan Brown cannily extrapolates major plotlines for *The Solomon Key* from this locale. As ever, though, his cleverly woven web of pseudo-historical facts and fiction falls apart when subjected to any degree of rational analysis.

As previously discussed, it is virtually impossible that the Knights Templar arrived from Jerusalem, via France, bearing treasure from beneath King Solomon's Temple. Furthermore, in their 2005 book *Rosslyn and the Grail*, historians Mark Oxbrow and Ian Robertson identify the Sinclairs as devout Catholics rather than Templars, and interpret the Chapel's decorations as simply traditional Christian (and Arthurian) iconography, including biblical scenes like the crucifixion, bereft of links to Freemasonry.

'The whole chapel is completely straightforward,' Oxbrow said in 2005. 'If people continue to fictionalize history it's a bad thing, not least because the real stories are more interesting. Anything about the Templars [at Rosslyn] is just rubbish built on sand.'

Even the United Grand Lodge of England, in the person of former Librarian and Curator (1993–99) the Very Worshipful John Hamill, dismisses the idea that a handful of symbols at Rosslyn Chapel prove a link between the Knights Templar and modern Freemasonry. There are certainly mysteries attached to Rosslyn Chapel but, once again, Dan Brown's revisionist and sensationalist manipulation of such material merely muddies the waters.

2) AMERICA WAS A MASONIC PROJECT

Dan Brown makes further guerrilla raids on the theories of alternative historians Knight and Lomas for the attention-grabbing Big Idea of *The Solomon Key* – that the United States possesses an incredible 'hidden history' and that both Freemasonry and the Knights Templar are not just implicated in, but largely responsible for, the birth of America.

Welcome to America: the Pre-Columbus Templars?

In *The Second Messiah: Templars, the Turin Shroud and the Great Secret of Freemasonry*, Knight and

Lomas argue that both the Essenes and another ancient Jewish sect named the Mandaeans had a mystical awareness of the existence of America even before Christ: '*[They] believed that good souls reside beyond the ocean to the west ... this wonderful place is marked by a star called Merica, that sits in the sky above it.*'

The Second Messiah's theorizing holds that the Knights Templar stumbled across this inspired premonition amongst the manuscripts they discovered on Mount Moriah (or, as Brown prefers, amongst the 'Sangreal documents' of *The Da Vinci Code*). The authors suggest that after the Catholic suppression of 1307, some fleeing Templars thus headed not for Scotland but across the Atlantic:

'We believe that this star and the mythical land below it were known to the Knights Templar from the scrolls that they discovered, and that they sailed in search of 'La Merica' or, as we now know it, America, immediately after their Order had been outlawed.'

This radical rewriting of the timeline of American history would have the Knights Templar landing on the East Coast of the US a full 185 years before Christopher Columbus disembarked in 1492. Yet exponents of this bizarre theory believe they are vindicated by evidence in one of Dan Brown's very favourite locales – Rosslyn Chapel.

Dr Lomas claims that the Chapel, completed six years before Columbus set sail, bears carved representations of plants like aloe and maize native only to the Americas – indicating that the Templars had not only discovered the US but had then sailed back to rejoin their low-profile colleagues in Scotland! He also cites the existence of early graves in Nova Scotia (which, of course, means New Scotland) bearing Templar and Masonic symbols.

This evidence seems flimsy in the extreme. The Nova Scotia iconography is ambiguous and impossible to date precisely, and while the Knights Templar may have been famously discreet, it stretches credulity beyond known limits to imagine they discovered a vast continent, returned to Europe and gave no indication of their adventure beyond a tiny cryptic carving inside a Scottish chapel! Fact may be stranger than fiction but this particular position appears untenable.

New Ideas for a New Land

While it is demonstrably ludicrous to suggest that Templar/Masonic figures discovered America almost 200 years before Columbus, Dan Brown is on more productive soil with the contention that the philosophy and ethics of Freemasonry helped to shape the United States in its formative years of independence. To explain why, we need to set a little historical context.

European Freemasonry was a maelstrom of progressive thinking in the early seventeenth century. Freed from unthinking subservience to the Church – Catholic *or* Protestant – rationalists and scientists like Robert Moray, Sir Christopher Wren and Elias Ashmole used speculative Freemasonry as a forum to discuss the best way to perfect their own natures and society.

In England, philosopher, scientist and statesman Sir Francis Bacon wrote a utopian tract called *The New Atlantis*, which remained unfinished when he died in 1626. The book, telling the tale of a land wherein faith and reason co-exist in perfect balance with mysticism, was profoundly influenced by a new cult that had arisen in Germany – the Rosicrucians.

The purported founder of the Rosicrucians was one Christian Rosenkreuz, a fourteenth-century German monk who had travelled through the Holy Lands gathering esoteric knowledge from spiritual leaders. Posthumous tracts written by this 'Rosenkreuz' appeared in 1614 and 1615 and used allegory and mystical symbolism to signpost a path towards moral and spiritual self-improvement.

The Rosicrucians were the philosophical fad of the mid-seventeenth century, as not just Bacon but also Isaac Newton, Ludwig van Beethoven and Leonardo Da Vinci were initiated into the order. Hundreds of leading speculative Freemasons also joined – indeed, at one stage it was believed that it was Rosenkreuz who had absorbed the wisdom of Solomon from descendants of the Dionsyian Artificers and passed it on to Freemasonry.

Ironically, Rosenkreuz was a hoax. The wandering monk was a figment of the imagination of one Johann Valentin Andrae, a German Lutheran minister who wanted a mystical figurehead for a movement stressing faith, reason and scientific

* * * * * * * *

The Rosenkreuz Myth

It's easy to see why Andrae's carefully cultivated Rosenkreuz myth chimed with seventeenth century Freemasonry. Rosenkreuz was said to have accumulated secret wisdom in the Biblical Lands before returning to Germany where he formed an order of monks based in the House of Holy Spirit, or Spiritus Sanctum. Andrae's legend claimed that Rosenkreuz died in 1484 aged 106 and was buried in a crypt in the house. When a monk accidentally disturbed the crypt in 1604, Rosenkreuz's body lay immaculately preserved alongside 'Book M' – a vast tome written by King Solomon himself.

* * * * * * * *

inquiry as tools towards utopian perfection in society. Late in his life, a remorseful Andrae confessed his well-intentioned deception, but even after this Rosicrucianism retained an elevated currency.

As many Freemasons departed to start a new life in America in the early eighteenth century, they took the utopian ideas of Rosicrucianism with them. With Britain still exerting colonial rule over the nascent States, Dan Brown argues that these powerful ex-pats resolved to create a real-life utopia in the 'new territories' by making America a 'Masonic Republic' – a claim that suits his novelistic purposes but is undoubtedly vastly exaggerated.

A Masonic Revolution?

There is no doubt some American Masons, especially those of a Rosicrucian inclination, were keen to cut colonial ties with London and craft America as a utopian, democratic idyll. Nevertheless, many ex-pat Masons – especially in military lodges – were traditionalists who remained fiercely patriotic. They would also have been mindful that Anderson's Book of Constitutions forbade any insurgency against public authorities.

Even the famous claim that the Boston Tea Party was the work of masked men from St Andrew's Lodge at the Green Dragon (see page 61) is open to doubt. St Andrew's Lodge *was* meeting

* * * * * * * *

Warren, Revere and Hancock

The American Revolution may not have been a Masonic exercise but three members of St Andrew's Lodge aided its inception. Having been in the gang that boarded the English clippers at the Boston Tea Party, Paul Revere then rode a horse to New York to carry the news. Joseph Warren died a hero's death at Bunker Hill, and John Hancock was a signatory to the Declaration of Independence.

* * * * * * * *

at the bar that day but so were a radical anti-British group named the Sons of Liberty, who were far more likely to adopt confrontational measures.

Founding A Nation

Dan Brown's *The Solomon Key* proposition that the United States has a hidden history as a Masonic republic is partly predicated on the number of known Freemasons who played a part in the

Revolution, became Founding Fathers or – in the most famous case of all – America's first President. There is no shortage of material for Brown to draw upon.

Benjamin Franklin was a Pennsylvania Grand Lodge Grand Master, in 1734, at the age of 28. Originally a printer then a newspaper owner, he published Anderson's Book of Constitutions in America. In 1757 he moved to England where he defended American interests and advised King George III against imposing prohibitive taxes on the colony.

Franklin returned to America during the War of Independence and helped to draft the Declaration of Independence. Known Freemasons who signed the Declaration included John Hancock, Joseph Hewes, William Hooper, Robert Payne, Richard Stockton, George Walton and William Whipple, while a further seven signatories – including Thomas Jefferson – were believed to be Masonic members or sympathisers.

Revisionist Masonic historians have argued that as many as fifty Declaration of Independence signatories were Freemasons, but there is no evidence that this was the case – nor, indeed, that

* * * * * * * *

Franklin in France

Posted to France as America's first ambassador to that territory in 1776, Benjamin Franklin joined a Parisian Masonic lodge known as the *Loge de Neuf Soeurs* (Lodge of Nine Sisters). Fellow members included American revolutionary hero Gilbert Lafayette, French man of letters and folk hero Voltaire and several figures who, a decade later, were closely involved in the French Revolution.

* * * * * * * *

4 July was chosen as Independence Day to mark the date that the Knights Templar were driven from Jerusalem by Muslim armies in 1187! Likewise, Dan Brown is not the first observer to comment on the high percentage of Freemasons among America's Founding Fathers.

Brown fails, however, to separate cause from effect. As in Paris ten years later, the Freemasons were regarded as a superior debating and philosophical society in British-ruled America – it is no surprise that progressive thinkers tended

* * * * * * * *

George Washington the Mason

Born in 1723, George Washington joined a local lodge in Fredericksburg, Virginia aged 21 and became a Master Mason just one year later. While never hugely active in the fraternity, he valued Masonic ideals, describing them as the 'cement that binds us together'. A year after becoming the first President of the United States in 1787, he agreed to become an honorary Grand Master of Alexandria Lodge in Washington DC.

* * * * * * * *

to be members. Yet all evidence suggests that Freemasonry may have been a convenient crucible for the revolution, but it was not its driving force. Ultimately, the shared qualities of Masonic membership and the American Revolution were a belief in individuality, equality and justice.

3) WASHINGTON DC IS A MASONIC ROAD MAP

In *The Solomon Key*, Dan Brown perpetuates one of the most perplexing and truly preposterous anti-Masonic myths of all: that George Washington and America's founding fathers concealed various Masonic signs and symbolism within the design of the nation's capital, Washington DC.

George Washington and Thomas Jefferson hired French architect Pierre Charles L'Enfant (who, despite being a friend of Lafayette, does not appear to have been a Mason) to design a new federal capital in 1790. Before being fired for having a bad attitude, L'Enfant divided the city into four quadrants with the Capitol building at the centre. Diagonal avenues criss-cross this grid.

Over-active theorists' imaginations have spotted numerous possible Masonic references in Washington's design, the main ones being:

- the Capitol is the top of a Masonic compass, with its legs leading off to the White House and the Jefferson Memorial;
- North and East of the White House, the

intersection of five major avenues forms an inverted pentagram;

- octagonal patterns evocative of the symbol of the Knights Templar are scattered through the city.

It's hard to know where to begin the debunking of this fanciful notion. Firstly, Washington was the only Freemason involved in the creation of the capital city, and played no active part in its design. Secondly, the pentagram – inverted or otherwise – is a symbol with very little resonance in Masonry: indeed, it is more closely associated with Satanism. Thirdly, it is hard to conceive of America's Founding Fathers engaging in so juvenile and futile a large-scale pantomime. If the Masonic truth *is* out there, it certainly isn't hiding at the junction of Rhode Island Avenue and K Street NW.

4) AMERICA HAS A MASONIC EMBLEM

In *The Solomon Key*, Robert Langdon finds great significance in supposed Masonic imagery within the Great Seal of America (and, therefore, on the back of the American dollar). Dan Brown is less keen to acknowledge that this particular old chestnut is misleading – and easily cleared up.

The front of the Great Seal shows an eagle carrying thirty-two feathers. The eagle symbolizes John the Evangelist, a patron saint of Free-masonry. There are thirty-two degrees in Scottish Rite Masonry. The eagle also carries an olive branch, which is often linked with King Solomon, and above its head are thirteen stars seemingly arranged in the Star of David, or Seal of Solomon, and a Latin phrase, *E Pluribus Unum* ('One out of many'), heavily redolent of Masonry.

The back of the Seal depicts an All-Seeing Eye inside a triangle, a symbol used by Masons to represent the Great Architect of the Universe, hovering over an unfinished Egyptian pyramid – again, a Solomon reference? Under the pyramid, a Latin slogan reads *Novus Ordo Seclorum* – 'A new order of the ages', which some interpret as a reference to the supposed Masonic wish to establish a New World Order.

However, all of these allegations are easily re-futable. The bald eagle was selected as America's emblem in 1782 as a symbol of strength and longevity – and because it was believed at the time

* * * * * * * *

The Secrets of the Seal

The attempts to read huge Masonic significance into the Great Seal can go to extraordinary lengths. Esoteric writer Greg Taylor argues that if a hexagram, or Seal of Solomon, is laid over the reverse of the Seal, its six points connect with five letters: M, A, S, O and N. The sixth point forms the apex of the All-Seeing Eye.

* * * * * * * *

to be native only to the US. The olive branch is a universal symbol of peace, while the thirteen stars represent the thirteen original states being joined as one: *E Pluribus Unum*. The idea of thirty-two feathers being a hidden code for the Scottish Rite merely seems contrived, especially as the Rite actually has thirty-three degrees (see Chapter 3: Inside the Lodge Masonic Rituals and Symbols).

The All-Seeing Eye, which Dan Brown links to eighteenth century German sect the Illuminati, is a visual symbol for God that dates from the Renaissance – the triangle around it represents the Holy Trinity. Pyramids, likewise, are often used as visual notation for a mighty building process, while *Novus Ordo Seclorum* is a fitting slogan for an emerging great nation.

Most tellingly of all, no Freemasons were involved in meaningful design of the Great Seal. The ubiquitous Benjamin Franklin worked on an initial draft that was rejected in 1776, but after that three different committees saw their ideas modified or knocked back by Congress before the final Great Seal was passed six years later. There was not a single Mason on any committee.

5) THE MASONIC NEW WORLD ORDER

Ever since Freemasonry's inception, there has been no shortage of enemies of the fraternity keen to condemn it as a cabal of clandestine plotters seeking to overthrow Church and State bodies across the globe and establish a New World Order.

Some damage was done to Masonry by its perceived association with a body called the Illuminati (Enlightened Ones). Formed in Bavaria in 1776 (some conspiracy theorists even believe the use of this date on the Grand Seal of America is significant) by a Mason called Adam Weishaupt, this elite secret society actually *was* dedicated to toppling corrupt elected governments everywhere to replace them with a perfect, totally virtuous global authority.

The Illuminati used Masonic-style ceremonies in their degree rituals but had effectively died out by the end of the eighteenth century. Despite this, the legend persists in some ill-informed circles that Freemasonry remains driven by Machiavellian motivations of eventual world domination.

Anti-Masonic writers Ivan Fraser and Mark Beeston claim that Freemasonry is controlled by 'modern Illuminati' who function at the highest levels of the global military-industrial hierarchy. However, it is hard to envisage Masonry mounting a dastardly assault on civilized society as we know it. Coordinating the campaign may prove difficult for a fraternity that not only has no worldwide organization, but in which competing Grand Lodges often refuse even to recognize each other.

* * * * * * * *

Snuffing Out The Illuminati

Weishaupt's Illuminati (originally called the Order of Perfectionists) never attracted more than a few hundred members across Northern Europe, and died out when Weishaupt fled Bavaria in 1784 as the government were poised to arrest him for plotting sedition and treason. This has only added to the sect's intrigue and lustre amongst the credulous – even in 2005, a US television show claimed that not only do the Illuminati still exist, they now possess weapons of mass destruction!

* * * * * * * *

Fundamentalist Christian groups, angered by Masonry's perceived Deism, have in recent years also accused Freemasonry of harbouring plans for world domination. Notorious US television evangelist Pat Robertson summarized this askew argument in 1991 in his splendidly barking book *The New World Order* – Dan Brown aficionados may be pleased to know their literary hero is keeping such good philosophical company.

6) MASONIC DEVIL WORSHIP

In the late nineteenth century a myth arose that Freemasons worshipped Lucifer within the walls of local lodges. This notion was entirely the handiwork of the greatest Masonic hoaxer of all time – one Leo Taxil.

Born Gabriel Jogand-Pagès in Marseilles in 1854, Taxil wrote anti-Catholic tracts before turning his fire on the Freemasons, who had kicked him out of a lodge at Entered Apprentice stage for perceived character faults. Using his (limited) knowledge of Masonic ritual, Taxil wrote a series of sensationalist 'exposés' of the fraternity. They were also utter fabrications.

Taxil claimed that Masonic scholar Albert Pike, the founder of the Scottish Rite, secretly presided over a Masonic discipline called Palladism whose members engaged in sexual orgies and worshipped Lucifer and Baphomet – allegations that were remarkably similar to the charges levelled by Paris and Rome at the Knights Templar in 1307.

Despite Taxil's previous history of maligning Catholicism, his accusations found favour with

* * * * * * * *

Baphomet

King Philip IV of France and Pope Clement V accused the Knights Templar of worshipping Baphomet, a talking head that lived deep beneath Mount Moriah. In Leo Taxil's propaganda, this arcane deity had become a half-male, half-female goat-like creature with a pentagram on its forehead, while in *The Da Vinci Code* Robert Langdon describes Baphomet as 'a pagan fertility god associated with the creative forces of reproduction'. The Baphomet legend also part-explains a great British urban myth of the 1950s – that Freemasons regularly rode goats around the lodge naked during their degree rituals.

* * * * * * * *

Pope Leo XII, who lapped up books like *The Anti-Christ and the Origin of Masonry* and *The Masonic Assassins*. Much like Dan Brown over a century later, Taxil's convoluted imaginings of 'hidden histories' struck a populist nerve – and made him absurdly wealthy.

Taxil confessed (or, rather, boasted of) his

fictions in 1897 and retired to count his money, but this minor fact has not prevented conspiracy theorists and Christian fundamentalists drawing on his febrile fabrications as proof of Freemasonry's diabolic bent.

7) THE MASONS ARE A JEWISH CONSPIRACY

At the end of the nineteenth century the Russian secret police unveiled a manifesto called The Protocols of the Elders of Zion. This notorious – and completely fabricated – document claimed that Jews and Freemasons covertly controlled the international banking system plus the judiciary and press of nearly every nation extant, and were hell-bent on eventual world domination.

The deliberately provocative Protocols led to anti-Jewish pogroms after the 1917 Russian revolution and had a further terrible echo in Nazi Germany, where Hitler banned all Masonic lodges in Germany in 1935 as a response to the ongoing perceived 'Judeo-Masonic world conspiracy'. Within two years, Freemasons were

* * * * * * * *

Masons Not Welcome

The belief that Masonry is implicated in a Jewish plan to establish a New World Order is one of the most entrenched of all anti-Masonic conspiracy theories. It led to the movement being banned in Hitler's Germany, Mussolini's Italy, Franco's Spain, Pinochet's Chile, Saddam Hussein's Iraq, and for the entire existence of the Soviet Union, where the Communist Party regarded lodges as 'meeting places for the adherents of Western imperialism'.

* * * * * * * *

being slaughtered in concentration camps alongside Jews.

Despite Freemasonry's adoption of King Solomon's Temple as its central image, there are no formal links between Masonry and Judaism. However, historically this has not prevented the fraternity being banned by fascist regimes where anti-Israeli feelings hold sway – and, today, throughout most of the Middle East.

8) FREEMASONRY AND THE
KU KLUX KLAN

Some anti-Masonic organisations claim that there are historical connections between Freemasonry and US white supremacist groups such as the Ku Klux Klan. Clearly Masonry has in the past reflected some less-than-enlightened contemporary societal attitudes, as evidenced by the struggles of the Prince Hall Masons to obtain Grand Lodge Masonic recognition after the US War of Independence.

The KKK was founded in Tennessee in 1866 and its first Imperial Wizard, former Confederate general Nathan Bedford Forrest, was also a Freemason. Scottish Rite founder Albert Pike has also been accused of being a senior KKK figure, and when asked about mixed-race Masonry, famously replied: 'I took my obligation [to Freemasonry] to white men, not to Negroes. When I have to accept Negroes as brothers or leave Masonry, I shall leave it.'

Masonic scholars have questioned the claim that Pike was active in the KKK and explain his casual racism as simply typical of its time, adding

* * * * * * * *

Masonry and Racism

Freemasonry Watch (www.freemasonrywatch.org) claims KKK meetings were held in US Masonic lodges in the 1930s and alleges the memberships of both organizations in certain areas were 'indistinguishable'. It also points to segregationist Deep South politicians like Alabama's Senator George Wallace being active Masons during the 1960s civil rights struggles, and reports a Freemason in Oklahoma resigning as late as 1999 because 'racism is rampant' in his lodge.

* * * * * * * *

that he opposed slavery and was well disposed towards Prince Hall Masonry. While Freemasonry today remains overwhelmingly white, only the most fervent anti-Masonic agitators would accuse it of residual racism.

9) JACK THE RIPPER WAS A MASON

In Britain in the 1970s, an outlandish book called *Jack The Ripper: The Final Solution* by anti-Masonic author Stephen Knight floated the idea that the infamous Victorian prostitute murders in London's East End had been committed by a high-ranking Freemason – Dr William Gull, a doctor at the court of Queen Victoria.

Knight's bizarre tome claimed the septuagenarian medic had murdered five ladies of the night in the gruesome manner proscribed by early Masonic degrees as punishment for Masons who betrayed the Craft – some had been garrotted, others disembowelled. Even more preposterously, he alleged the killings were at the express command of Queen Victoria herself!

Knight also read great significance into graffiti that had appeared on a wall by one victim: 'The Juwes [sic] are the men that will not be blamed for nothing'. Far from being anti-Jewish sloganeering, Knight alleged it was a reference to the 'Juwes' – Jubelo, Jubela and Jubelum – who murdered Hiram Abiff, and claimed a Masonic/

Establishment cover-up had occurred over the Ripper deaths.

Sadly, the author neglected to consider that not only did Hiram Abiff's killers loudly blame themselves for his death – they also nominated their own severe punishments before being gruesomely put to death. As conspiracy theories go, this was a spectacular non-starter.

10) FREEMASONRY IS A HOTBED OF CRONYISM

For all of the far-fetched conspiracy theories thrown at Freemasons, the most accurate is probably the most mundane – that Masons can be heavily prone to nepotism and favouritism towards each other outside of the lodge, and that local lodges function as elaborate, role-playing old boys' clubs.

One of the many oaths taken by Freemasons is a pledge never to use their membership of the movement for personal gain, or to favour fellow lodge members over non-Masons. Human nature being as it is, however, a fair degree of cronyism is inevitable, and there have been numerous instances of Mason-related corruption among business and civic leaders over the years.

In a major scandal in 1977, London police chiefs and detectives who were linked by Masonry were found guilty of extorting money, planting evidence on innocent men and accepting bribes from the main players in London's sex trade – some coppers even initiated pornographers into their local lodge! Thirteen CID detectives were jailed at the end of an explosive and, for Freemasonry, highly damaging trial at the Old Bailey.

Nobody knows how prevalent such practises remain, but eager anti-Masonic zealots such as former TV presenter David Icke chronicle any new examples of Masonry-connected corruption at conspiracy theory-heavy websites like www.david icke.com and www.davidicke.net. *Private Eye* also occasionally brings such instances to light. In truth, planning permissions passed on a nod and a wink may not be as enthralling to Dan Brown as convoluted strategies incorporating the Dionysian Artificers of Tyre, but they remain the anti-Freemasonic allegations with the most relevance and currency.

* * * * * * * *

The Bilderberg Group

While not actually a Masonic organization, the Bilderberg Group is seen in some quarters as the most sinister and clandestine secret society of all. Founded in 1954 by Prince Bernhard of Holland, the Group brings together the world's most powerful figures on an annual basis. Media coverage is scant and the conversational agenda is kept secret, but attendees in recent years have included Presidents George H.W. Bush, Bill Clinton and George W. Bush, British Prime Ministers Margaret Thatcher, John Major and Tony Blair, as well as Donald Rumsfeld, Bill Gates, David Rockefeller, Conrad Black, The Observer editor Will Hutton, former UK Green Party leader Jonathan Porritt ... and even Stephen Spielberg. For advanced level anti-Bilderberg theorizing, see www.bilderberg.org.

* * * * * * * *

INSIDE THE LODGE -
MASONIC RITUALS AND
SYMBOLS

'What have you come here to do?'
'To learn to subdue my passions, and improve
myself in Masonry.'
　An opening exchange of the Entered
　Apprentice degree.

The lodge is the main building-brick of Freemasonry – the word means both any local chapter
of Masons, and the building wherein they meet.
These buildings may be unprepossessing on the
outside, but inside are laid out in ornate splendour
according to the strict conditions of the Craft.

Masonic lodges are rectangular and are ideally
aligned from east to west to mirror the path of the
sun, as were the ancient temples. Even when this
is not practically possible, the inner windowless

* * * * * * * *

The First Lodges

The word lodge is derived from the French loge, which originally meant a hut or temporary structure erected by medieval stonemasons next to their building site. This temporary HQ was a base for the workers to rest, eat and sleep overnight when working away from home.

* * * * * * * *

chamber of the lodge, where all meetings and degree ceremonies are held, faces towards the east – if not physically, then at least symbolically.

Each lodge is a symbolic representation of King Solomon's Temple and is decorated accordingly. The Worshipful Master sits to the east of the Lodge, on a seat raised three steps off the ground. In the west is the Senior Warden raised up two steps, while the Junior Warden sits to the south, elevated just one step from the ground.

There are chairs or benches for Masons to observe proceedings along the north and south walls of the lodge or, in some instances, around the whole perimeter. Behind the Senior Warden at the west end is a lockable door, through which all candidates for degree ceremonies enter and exit.

The floor of the lodge, which symbolizes the earth, is normally tiled in a black-and-white chessboard pattern, or some similar mosaic. The ceiling represents the 'canopy of heaven' and is generally heavily decorated with a moon, stars, clouds and various Masonic symbols.

Somewhere in the lodge stands an altar, which contains a holy book known in Freemasonry as the Volume of Sacred Law. This can be a Bible, a Koran or any sacred scripture, but must stand open while meetings are in progress to symbolically remind Masons of their duty of self-improvement. Three candles illuminate the Volume as it stands on the altar.

On either side of the Senior Warden's chair – or occasionally elsewhere in the lodge – stand two carved columns, normally bearing decorated globes on the top. These are direct representations of Jachin and Boaz, the bronze pillars that were a major structural feature of King Solomon's Temple.

The lodge's banner, usually five or six feet deep, will hang from a beam or a pole near the

* * * * * * * *

Three Great Lights

Always on display in Masonic lodge rooms, the Three Great Lights of Freemasonry are said to be the Volume of Sacred Law, the square and the compass.

Symbolically, their radiance and essence is said to reside in the lodge's three most senior officers: the Worshipful Master, Senior Warden and Junior Warden.

* * * * * * * *

Worshipful Master's seat. It contains the lodge's name, date of forming and number (awarded by UGLE) and a design related to the lodge's name or history, as well as complex Masonic symbols. These mini-tapestries are often splendidly intricate and detailed.

The square and compass, the definitive image of Freemasonry, (see illustration 1, page 128) will be displayed on the walls, possibly over the Worshipful Master's seat. Also visible will be a Tracing Board, a symbol-festooned canvas or board that reflects the particular degree ceremony being carried out by the meeting.

*   *   *   *   *   *   *   *

In The Key of G

In America, the Freemasonic square-and-compass image
has been modified so that the tools enclose a letter G.
This letter symbolizes both the Great Architect of the
Universe and also Geometry, the founding science of
Masonry. In US lodges this icon is normally illuminated
and hangs over the Worshipful Master's chair.

*   *   *   *   *   *   *   *

The Tracing Board is a hangover from eighteenth
century Masonry, when lodges had no meeting-
rooms but instead convened in rooms over
taverns. Originally they would daub Masonic

slogans on the floor in chalk before progressing to an icon-covered cloth that they hung over an easel - a tradition that continues today.

Most lodges meet once a month to discuss routine business, plan charitable events, consider details of potential new members and socialize. They may also hear presentations from members or visitors from other lodges about an aspect of Masonic history or tradition.

Regular meetings can be held with only three members present, but at least seven of the lodge's officers - or their temporary replacements - are needed for degree ceremonies. These ritual offices are held by elected or selected Master Masons from within the lodge, who then spend one year in each post before progressing further up the hierarchical chain.

The Masonic Seating Plan

Worshipful Master

The most senior position in the lodge, the Worshipful Master, presides over all lodge business and degree ceremonies from his seat to the east of the lodge, symbolic of the rising sun. Charged with 'setting the Craft to work and giving them good and wholesome instruction for their labour', other presidential duties including overseeing internal elections and representing the lodge at the annual meetings of the Grand Lodge that it is affiliated to. The Worshipful Master formally opens and closes the lodge at meetings and is the pivotal figure in all initiation ceremonies, for which he has to learn vast swathes of text by rote in order to quiz the candidate.

SENIOR WARDEN

Second-in-command to the Worshipful Master, the Senior Warden sits in the west of the lodge, representing the setting sun, and assists the WM in all areas of running the lodge. The Senior Warden spends a lot of his year in the post learning the duties of the Master and memorizing Masonic ritual, and is expected to be able to fill in for the WM any time that he is absent.

JUNIOR WARDEN

Sitting in the south of the lodge to represent the position of the workday sun at noon, the Junior

* * * * * * * *

The Wardens Have Wood

The Senior and Junior Wardens sit behind two small desks or posts each bearing a wooden column. While the lodge is meeting, the Senior Warden's column is upright to illustrate that he is in authority over the assembled Masons, while the Junior Mason lays his on its side. This arrangement is reversed at the meeting's end when the Craftsmen repair to the Festive Board organized by the Junior Mason.

* * * * * * * *

Warden assists the two senior officers and is responsible for many practical tasks around the lodge. He is often the first port of call for members who have issues or grievances, and is responsible for providing refreshments for the post-meeting meal known as the Festive Board. The Junior Warden opens and closes the lodge in the event of the Worshipful Master and Senior Warden being simultaneously absent.

SENIOR DEACON

The Senior Deacon sits to the right of the Worshipful Master in the lodge and is effectively his messenger. His duties include welcoming visiting Masons from other lodges plus opening and closing the Volume of Sacred Law and lighting and extinguishing candles at the start and end of meetings. During degree ceremonies the Senior Deacon guides candidates around the lodge and acts as a prompt should they forget their lines.

JUNIOR DEACON

Sitting to the right of the Senior Warden, the Junior Deacon generally assists the Senior Deacon but has the specific responsibility of ensuring that nobody enters or leaves the lodge room during a meeting unless specifically allowed to do so by the Worshipful Master. The Junior Deacon also helps candidates to prepare for their degree ceremonies and, like the Senior Deacon, carries a rod modelled on that carried by the Roman god Mercury, to indicate they are messengers.

Inner Guard

The Junior Deacon is also known as the Inner Guard, and in very large lodges the Inner Guard is sometimes a separate post in its own right. The Mason who holds this office is primarily charged with assisting the Junior Deacon.

Senior Steward

The Senior Steward sits amongst the Craftsmen along the side of the room during lodge meetings and is a mere observer during initiation ceremonies. His role involves helping to arrange the lodge room before meetings and general dogsbody work, which may include waiting tables and helping the senior officers to discharge their duties between meetings if required.

Junior Steward

Sitting alongside the Senior Steward during meetings, the Junior Steward occupies the lowliest officer position in the lodge and his remit extends to little more than aiding the Senior Steward plus assisting the Junior Warden at the Festive Board. However, the Stewards are the only other Freemasons apart from the Deacons to carry rods – in

* * * * * * * *

Blue Lodge

A Masonic lodge that awards the basic three Entered Apprentice, Fellow Craft and Master Mason degrees is sometimes known as a Blue Lodge (or, alternatively, a Symbolic Lodge). The term is thought to originate from the blue ceiling in most lodges, representing the 'canopy of the heavens'.

* * * * * * * *

their case markedly similar to the one wielded by Black Rod in the House of Lords.

It is usual for a Mason selected for office to spend one year in each of these roles, meaning it will take him seven years to progress from Junior Steward to Worshipful Master – the same time as it took a stonemason to go from Entered Apprentice to Master Mason. However, there are other posts within the lodge apart from this process, which may be occupied for far longer.

Tyler

Also known as the Outer Guard, the Tyler stands outside the locked door of the lodge with a sword during meetings to prevent unwelcome intrusions. The Tyler ensures that all lodge visitors are correctly clothed – indeed, some lodges make washing the aprons one of his duties! Once the meeting has started the Tyler admits tardy Masons at his own discretion, communicating with the Junior Deacon or Inner Guard via knocks on the closed door. His sword has no sheath and is always drawn – symbolizing eternal vigilance.

Secretary

Sitting to the left of the Worshipful Master during meetings, the secretary carries out a host of administrative functions including taking minutes, keeping the members' register up to date and answering all post.

Treasurer

The lodge Treasurer sits behind the Senior Deacon and handles all financial matters for the lodge, including preparing regular statements of account.

* * * * * * * *

Cowans and Lions

Masonic tradition has it that the Tyler guards the lodge room from 'cowans and eavesdroppers'. In medieval times, cowans were unregulated builders excluded from stonemasons' guilds for poor work or bad attitude. The Tyler ensured these rogue workmen did not overhear the Masons' trade secrets. He was also, bizarrely, charged with protecting the lodge against wild animals.

* * * * * * * *

CHAPLAIN

The Chaplain sits next to the Secretary during meetings and does not need to be an ordained religious minister outside of the lodge. His duties are to read the non-denominational prayers that open and close meetings and do the same during degree ceremonies. He also takes care of the Volume of Sacred Law, which, despite Freemasonry's non-Christian-specific nature, is nearly always the King James Bible in British and American lodges.

DIRECTOR OF CEREMONIES

The Director of Ceremonies' role is hard to define except to say that it is his business to ensure that all meetings run successfully, fluidly and in line with Masonic rules and tradition. Of course, these are primarily the Worshipful Master's responsibilities, but the Director of Ceremonies acts as both his guide (if required) and his batman in meetings. Traditionally, this role is often filled by a former Grand Master of the lodge.

ALMONER

Larger lodges will elect a Mason to the post of Almoner and he will be in charge of maintaining contact between the lodge and members who are absent due to sickness, travelling or family circumstances. It is his particular duty to coordinate efforts to give assistance to this Mason – financial or spiritual – if appropriate, and to liaise with any external charitable bodies who may be contacted to help him.

CHARITY STEWARD

The Charity Steward handles all other charitable activities that the lodge may engage in. This involves organizing collections during monthly meetings, organizing fund-raising events and, together with the treasurer, arranging any charitable donations to good causes.

Organist
If there is one amongst their number, some lodges employ the services of an organist to play music to open and close the meetings, and occasionally during degree ceremonies.

Immediate Past Master
The hierarchical structure of Masonic lodges and the annual promotion system of moving from level to level means that when a Worshipful Master's term of office finishes, there is nowhere for this venerable figure to go except to return to the main body of the lodge. It is not permitted for him once again to ascend through the ranks for a 'second lap'.

However, some lodges ask the retiring Worshipful Master to spend a further year in the role of Immediate Past Master. Effectively a lodge sage, the IPM is a grandee without specific duties whose sole role is to make available if requested his experience and knowledge of Masonic history and ritual to the new Worshipful Master. This elder statesman is not permitted to deputize for absent senior officers or to play any formal role during meetings unless he is acting as the Director of Ceremonies.

Nevertheless, the Immediate Past Master remains well respected within the lodge, and is rewarded for his past achievements with the honorary title Worshipful Brother and the initials PM appended to his name. A few US lodges also allow Past Masters to continue to vote at meetings.

Former Worshipful Masters may also be voted into the organizational structure of the local Grand Lodge, which meets once per year apart from in exceptional circumstances. Its chain of command proceeds in an identical manner to that of the local lodges – Junior Grand Steward, Senior Grand Steward, Junior Grand Deacon, etc – culminating in the Most Worshipful Grand Master.

The dress code for Freemasons attending lodge meetings is strictly formal, with most lodges requiring their members to wear a dark suit, white shirt, black tie, black shoes and black socks. A few ultra-traditionalist lodges even insist on morning suits, and white gloves are universally compulsory. However, there is no doubting the most important item of Masonic attire – the apron.

All Masons, from the Worshipful Master down to the Entered Apprentices, wear an apron at all times while inside the lodge room. The Tyler is charged not to admit anybody to the room who is not wearing an apron, with the sole exception of candidates arriving for their Entered Apprentice degree ceremonies.

The Masonic apron

The Freemasons' apron is rich with symbolism and significance. It harks back to both the genuine and the notional history of Masonry; medieval stonemasons wore aprons to protect their clothes and carry their work tools, but Masonic theory also holds that workmen in King Solomon's Temple were similarly attired. History reports that the Knights Templar also wore aprons as part of their monastic uniform.

Originally made of lambskin, but nowadays more often of thick cloth, the white Masonic apron symbolises purity of thought and deed. It's significant that in Masonic legend, the plotters against Hiram Abiff who decided not to go through with the attack went before King Solomon wearing white aprons to represent the fact that they were innocent of his murder.

Masons are given their aprons during the course of the Entered Apprentice degree. Initially they are plain white with a thin blue border, symbolizing that the new Mason is now a member of a Blue Lodge. When he becomes a Fellow Craft two blue rosettes are stitched on the lower corners. A third is added, this time to the triangular flap that hangs from the top of the apron, when he graduates to a Master Mason. Two metal tassels are also added at this stage.

The aprons become more ornate and decorated if a Mason ascends to lodge office. Each post within the lodge traditionally has it own Masonic jewel of office, and these tools are sewn onto the appropriate officer's apron (they also wear the same tools on chains around their necks). The jewels of office are:

Worshipful Master	Right-angled square
Senior Warden	Level
Junior Warde	Plumb
Senior Deacon [see Note 1]	Square and compass with a sun in the centre
Junior Deacon [see Note 1]	Square and compass with a moon in the centre
Inner Guard	Two swords in saltire
Senior / Junior Stewards	Horn of plenty
Tyler	Sword
Secretary	Crossed pens in saltire
Treasurer	Key or crossed keys
Chaplain	Opened book
Director of Ceremonies	Two rods in saltire tied with a ribbon
Almoner	Scrip-purse bearing a heart
Charity steward	Trowel
Organist	Lyre
Past Master [see Note 2]	Compass

THE MASONIC DEGREE CEREMONIES

Ever since the Middle Ages, when stonemasons' guilds met in secret and the medieval security guard known as the Tyler saw off the attentions of cowans and eavesdroppers, the activities carried out within the walls of a Masonic lodge have been shrouded in mystery and intrigue. At the centre of this mystique lie the Blue Lodge degree ceremonies – an extraordinary cocktail of bizarre costumes, ritualistic catechisms, call-

---

NOTES

1) In some lodges the Deacons have an alternative jewel of office of a dove bearing an olive branch

2) Many American lodges mark Freemasonry's Pythagorean roots by awarding Past Masters a more complex jewel: a geometric device known as the 47th Proposition of Euclid engraved on a silver plate. It represents the complex mathematical calculation better known as Pythagoras' Theorem: the square of the hypotenuse is equal to the sum of the square of the other two sides.

and-response routines and the re-enactment of a mysterious Biblical-era murder.

Freemasonry's insistence on these rituals remaining secret probably does the movement a disservice. The few snippets that do leak out to the outside world – tales of blindfolded middle-aged men with their trouser-legs rolled up being led around ceremoniously by a noose – appear so preposterous that Masonry is inevitably stripped in the public imagination of the respect it craves, being regarded instead as possessing the approximate gravitas and relevance to the twenty-first century of bear-baiting or dwarf-hurling.

There is no question that Masonic degree ceremonies are arcane and archaic, but much of their appeal to participants doubtless lies in their very exoticism and layers of seemingly impenetrable obfuscation. In the cause of greater wider understanding of Freemasonry's appeal, we will now dissect exactly what is said in Masonic degree rituals – and explain what it all means.

The language used in Masonic degrees has changed little in three centuries. Each degree consists of rigidly structured catechisms that the candidate must learn by rote. He must regurgitate these during the ceremony, although lodge officers will prompt him if he runs dry. The ceremonies also contain set moral lectures and lessons in Masonic history delivered by lodge officers.

Having made his interest known to his local lodge, a prospective candidate will be invited to apply for membership. The only requirements are that he must:

• be of legal age (18 in Britain, 21 in the US);
• have no criminal record;
• be of good moral character; and
• state belief in a Supreme Being and an afterlife.

Lodge members then investigate the individual's character before voting on whether to admit him in a brief internal election sometimes known as 'The Ordeal'. The Senior Deacon passes around the lodge with a wooden box and every member discreetly places a white or black ball in it.

The lodge will refuse the application if even one black ball is present when they are counted. However, given Freemasonry's worldwide declining membership, virtually all applicants nowadays are gratefully received and few suffer the humiliation of being 'black-balled'.

* * * * * * * *

The Three Degrees

Just as the lodge room is a scaled-down reconstruction of King Solomon's Temple, so the three 'Blue Lodge' degrees of Freemasonry are linked to progress through the Temple. The Entered Apprentice degree is said to represent the ground floor, the Fellow Craft the middle chamber, and the Master Mason ceremony the *Sanctum Sanctorum*. The three stages also stand for youth, manhood and old age. In Masonic parlance, a member is initiated as an Entered Apprentice, *passes* to Fellow Craft and is *raised* to a Master Mason.

* * * * * * * *

Once a lodge meeting has formally approved the application, an officer – usually the Junior Deacon – will meet the candidate and explain what is required of him at his Entered Apprentice examination, including giving him the catechism to learn. They will then set a date for his ceremonial first step into Freemasonry.

ENTERED APPRENTICE DEGREE

The Worshipful Master opens the meeting, asking the Deacons to confirm that all present in the lodge are Masons. He then asks each of the lodge's senior officers in turn to confirm their presence and purpose. This ritual is at the start of every degree ceremony, and the following excerpt of dialogue is typical:

WORSHIPFUL MASTER: 'Brother Senior Deacon.'

SENIOR DEACON: 'Worshipful Master?'

WORSHIPFUL MASTER: 'Your duty?'

SENIOR DEACON: 'To carry orders from the Worshipful Master in the East, to the Senior Warden in the West, and elsewhere about the Lodge as he may direct; welcome and clothe visiting Brethren, attend to alarms at the inner door; also to receive and conduct candidates.'

The Worshipful Master then declares the lodge open and the chaplain says non-denominational prayers (although they often tend to be highly Christian in flavour). At the end the members recite the Masonic version of Amen: *So mote it be*. The Senior Deacon displays the Three Great Lights

* * * * * * * *

Idiosyncrasies and Differences

The 1813 UGLE Reformation of Freemasonry allowed for local variations in the language used in degree ceremonies, and the precise phraseology varies between lodges. However, the transcriptions used here are essentially what is said at Masonic initiation ceremonies across the globe, give or take the odd passage.

* * * * * * * *

by opening the Volume of Sacred Law and lighting the candles around it.

The Worshipful Master then addresses the lodge: *'Brethren, Mr Jones is in waiting for the First Degree of Freemasonry, he having been duly accepted. If there is no objection, I shall confer this degree upon him.'* Having asked the Senior Steward how the candidate should be prepared, he is answered thus:

'By being divested of all metallic substances, neither naked nor clothed, barefoot nor shod, left knee and breast bare, hoodwinked and with a cable-tow about his neck.'

The Senior Steward and Secretary then repair to the ante-room where the candidate is waiting, and the Secretary asks him to swear that he understands the moral ethos of Freemasonry and will conform to its usages and customs. Having answered in the affirmative, he removes his street clothes and divests himself of money and all base metals – thereby symbolically losing all signs of wealth or social status. He also has to remove from his mind all 'passions and prejudices' before donning the supplied garments:

- a shirt with no left sleeve;
- a pair of trousers with no left leg;
- a shirt that is open over the heart;
- a slipper on his right foot and his left foot bare (this is known in Masonic parlance as being 'slipshod');
- a blindfold known as a hoodwink;
- a length of rope, or cable-tow, draped over his neck.

The bared flesh represents honesty and openness. The blindfold symbolizes that the candidate is in darkness until enlightened by Masonry. The cable-tow represents a willingness to learn: the trainee Apprentice is agreeing to be led by more experienced Craft members until he has absorbed their wisdom.

The Senior Steward leads the hoodwinked candidate by the cable-tow to the lodge door, where the Tyler checks he is properly attired. The candidate then knocks on the door, whereupon the following exchange occurs:

SENIOR DEACON: 'Who comes here?'

SENIOR STEWARD: 'Mr Jones, a poor blind candidate who is desirous of having and receiving a part in the rights, lights and benefits of this Worshipful Lodge of Free and Accepted Masons, as all Brethren and Fellows have done who have gone this way before him.'

SENIOR DEACON: 'Is this an act of your own free will and accord?'

Candidate: 'It is.'

SENIOR DEACON: 'Brother Stewards, is he worthy and well qualified?'

SENIOR STEWARD: 'He is.'

SENIOR DEACON: 'By what further right does he expect to obtain this important privilege?'

SENIOR STEWARD: 'Being a man, free born, of lawful age, and well recommended.'

The Senior Deacon asks permission of the

* * * * * * * *

Cable-Tow

The cable-tow was a length of rope that medieval stonemasons working high up a building used to pull their tools up from the ground. The rope's length also served as a measure of how high the Mason was willing to climb up the cathedral, or other structure being built, in the course of his duties.

* * * * * * * *

Worshipful Master for the candidate to enter the lodge. As soon as he does so, the Senior Deacon stands in front of him, holds a dagger to his chest, and says:

'Mr Jones, I am commanded to receive you on the point of a sharp instrument, piercing your naked left breast, which is to teach you that as this is an instrument of torture to the flesh, so should the recollection thereof be to your mind and conscience, should you ever reveal the secrets of Freemasonry unlawfully.'

The Senior Deacon then takes the cable-tow from the Senior Steward and leads the candidate to the centre of the lodge. As the assembled Masons stand, the new Apprentice kneels before the Worshipful Master, who says a short prayer for him.

There follows a process called circumambulation, whereby the Senior Deacon leads the candidate clockwise around the lodge assuring other senior lodge officers of his eligibility and suitability. The Senior Warden then instructs the candidate how to 'approach to East in due and ancient form': *'Mr Jones, advance on your left foot, bringing the heel of your right into the hollow of your left, thereby forming the angle of a square.'*

The Worshipful Master informs the candidate he must take an Obligation, assuring him it contains nothing that conflicts with the duties he owes to 'God, your country, your neighbour, your family or yourself', and orders him to assume the necessary position: *'Advance to the Sacred Altar of Freemasonry. There kneel on your naked left knee; your right knee forming the angle of a square; your left hand supporting, and your right hand resting on the Volume of Sacred Law, Square and Compasses.'*

Prompted by the Worshipful Master, the

candidate pledges to 'always hele, forever conceal and never reveal ... the hidden mysteries of Freemasonry'. At the end of the Obligation, the Worshipful Master tells the candidate to kiss the Volume of Sacred Law to prove his sincerity and the Senior Deacon removes the cable-tow from his shoulders.

WORSHIPFUL MASTER: 'My Brother, in your present situation, what do you most desire?'

CANDIDATE: 'Light in Masonry.'

The Worshipful Master recites a short prayer, which, in many lodges, ends with '*I say Masonic-ally – let there be light*'. As the Senior Deacon removes the new Apprentice's hoodwink, the whole lodge clap their hands once in unison and the Worshipful Master tells the candidate:

'*My Brother, on being brought to light in Free-masonry, you first behold the Three Great Lights, by aid of the representatives of the Three Lesser. The Three Great Lights in Masonry are the Volume of Sacred Law, Square and Compasses, and are thus explained: the Volume of Sacred Law is given us as the rule and guide for our faith and prac-tice, the Square to square our actions, and the Compasses circumscribe our desires and keep our*

* * * * * * * *

No More Tongue-Lashings

In a vague gesture towards modern sensibilities, English Freemasonry has diluted the apocalyptic threat to the Entered Apprentice candidate that, should he divulge the secrets of Freemasonry's secrets, he will (like Jubela) have 'my throat cut across, my tongue torn out, and my body buried in the sands of the sea at low-water mark, where the tide ebbs and flows, twice in twenty-four hours.' American Masonry, however, retains these colourful references to the punishments administered to the murderers of Hiram Abiff in all three of its Blue Lodge ceremonies.

* * * * * * * *

passions in due bound with all mankind, especially the Brethren.'

After a short moral homily, the Worshipful Master shows the new Mason the DUE-GUARD or stance of the Entered Apprentice: the heel of the right foot is placed into the hollow of the left to form the angle of a square, while the hands are once again positioned as if 'the left hand is *supporting the Volume of Holy Law and the right hand is resting thereon'* (see illustration 2, below).

Next, the Worshipful Master demonstrates the SIGN of the Entered Apprentice by drawing his right hand rapidly across his throat in a cutting motion then letting it drop to his side – a representation of the punishment that befell Jubela of

having his throat cut open and his tongue ripped out by its roots (see illustration 3, below).

The Worshipful Master then shakes the new Mason's hand, thereby teaching him the GRIP of the Entered Apprentice: both men press their thumbs against the knuckle-joint of the other man's first finger (see illustration 4, right). He

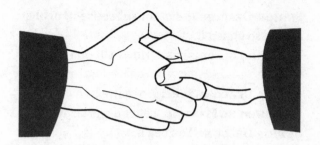

then co-opts the help of the Senior Deacon to teach the new apprentice the name of this grip:

WORSHIPFUL MASTER: 'Brother Senior Deacon.'

SENIOR DEACON: 'Worshipful Master.'

WORSHIPFUL MASTER: 'I hele.'

SENIOR DEACON: 'I conceal.'

WORSHIPFUL MASTER: 'What do you conceal?'

SENIOR DEACON: 'All the secrets of a Mason in Masonry, to which this alludes.'

WORSHIPFUL MASTER: 'What is that?'

SENIOR DEACON: 'A grip.'

WORSHIPFUL MASTER: 'Of what?'

SENIOR DEACON: 'Of an Entered Apprentice.'

WORSHIPFUL MASTER: 'Has it a name?'

SENIOR DEACON: 'It has.'

WORSHIPFUL MASTER: 'Will you give it to me?'

SENIOR DEACON: 'I did not so receive it, neither will I so impart it.'

WORSHIPFUL MASTER: 'How will you dispose of it?'

SENIOR DEACON: 'Letter it or halve it.'

WORSHIPFUL MASTER: 'Letter it and begin.'

SENIOR DEACON: 'You begin.'

WORSHIPFUL MASTER: 'Begin you.'

SENIOR DEACON: 'A.'

WORSHIPFUL MASTER: 'B.'

SENIOR DEACON: 'O.'

WORSHIPFUL MASTER: 'Z.'

The Worshipful Master then addresses the new Entered Apprentice: *'Boaz, my Brother, is the name of this grip, and should always be given in the customary manner, by lettering or halving. When lettering, always commence with the letter "A".'*

Having learned that the grip's name is BOAZ, after one of the two pillars in King Solomon's Temple, the new Entered Apprentice is prompted by the Senior Deacon to demonstrate his due-guard, sign and grip to the Junior and Senior Wardens.

The Worshipful Master then presents the new Entered Apprentice with his apron and gives

* * * * * * * *

The Dark Hand of Masonry?

During all Masonic degree ceremonies, the Senior Deacon explains the purpose of the secret grips by saying they are '… a certain friendly or brotherly grip, whereby one Mason may know another in the dark as in the light.' He also cryptically refers to their defining features as 'Right angles, horizontals and perpendiculars.'

* * * * * * * *

him the 'Apron Lecture' about its 'purity and perfection'. In some lodges, he may also tell him:

'I invest you with the distinguishing badge of a Mason. It is more ancient than the Golden Fleece or the Roman Eagle, more honourable than the Garter or any other Order in existence, being the badge of innocence and the bond of friendship.'

The Senior Warden tells him how it should be worn:

'My Brother, at the building of King Solomon's Temple the different brands of workmen were distinguished by the manner in which they wore their aprons. Entered Apprentices wore them with

> *the flap turned up to prevent soiling the clothing;*
> *Masonically, to prevent dubbing with untried*
> *mortar. Thus wear yours until further advanced.'*

The Worshipful Master then produces a collection plate and asks for a 'metallic substance', i.e. a charitable donation. The Apprentice has nothing, having been divested of his money before the ritual, so the Worshipful Master tells him to regard this as a lesson:

> *'Should you ever meet a member of the human*
> *family, especially a Brother Mason, in a like*
> *destitute situation, it would be your duty to con-*
> *tribute to his relief as liberally as his necessities*
> *might require, and your ability permits.'*

Next, the Worshipful Master presents the Apprentice with his 'working tools': the 24-inch gauge and the gavel. He explains their uses:

- Operative stonemasons used a gauge to measure bricks but the Entered Apprentice should use it figuratively to divide the twenty-four hours of the day: eight for work, eight for sleep, and eight for good works and giving thanks to the Great Architect of the Universe

- Just as stonemasons used the gavel to break off the corners of rough stone, so the Entered

Apprentice should hew from their minds all of the *'vices and superfluities of life'*.

The Senior Deacon then escorts the Apprentice to the northeast corner of the lodge room (traditionally, where a building's cornerstone is laid), and the Worshipful Master delivers the Entered Apprentice Lecture. He begins by dissecting the symbolism of the lodge, including the 'three supports' of the physical and spiritual edifice: wisdom, strength and beauty. (These are also linked to King Solomon, Hiram, King of Tyre and Hiram Abiff).

The Worshipful Master explains Freemasonry's movable (square, level, plumb) jewels before moving on to their immovable counterparts: the rough ashlar, perfect ashlar and trestle board. The rough ashlar (a hewed piece of stone) symbolizes the Entered Apprentice, while the perfect ashlar reflects the more sophisticated Fellow Craft. The trestle board traditionally held architect's diagrams and represents the wisdom of the Master Mason.

The lecture also covers the Mosaic Pavement (the chess-board floor, whose squares represent the challenges of everyday life) and the Indented

Tassel border standing for its rewards. The Worshipful Master also points out the icon of a five-pointed Blazing Star – a symbol of divine intervention.

In a more abstracted mode, the Worshipful Master next points the new Apprentice towards Masonry's major tenets of brotherly love, relief (i.e. empathy) and truth. He also extols Freemasonry's *'four cardinal virtues: Fortitude, Prudence, Temperance and Justice'*.

Finally, the Worshipful Master reads the Entered Apprentice Charge: the new Mason is 'charged' with honouring the Obligation, being a 'quiet and peaceable citizen' and studying the history, charges and regulation of the Craft. The Worshipful Master also appoints a Mason to help the Apprentice prepare for his next challenge: the Fellow Craft degree.

The Master closes the lodge with the same pomp and circumstance with which it opened, and members proceed to the Festive Board.

Festive Board

Arranged by the Junior Warden, the Festive Board takes place after most lodge meetings (or, occasionally, before). After a degree ceremony, it will traditionally feature complicated systems of toasts, synchronized single claps and songs. Some English lodges will end by singing the unofficial 'Masonic anthem', which is the national anthem, God Save the Queen, with two added verses:

'Hail! Mystic holy light
Heaven born and ever bright
Spread more and more;
Light of the bold and free,
Honour and loyalty,
Light of Freemasonry
Ne'er leave our shore.

Almighty Architect
Counsel, uphold, direct
Elizabeth our Queen;
Round her thy covering spread,
O'er her thy spirit shed,
Take her anointed head
Under Thy wing.'

FELLOW CRAFT DEGREE

There is no set time period that must lapse between a Mason taking the Entered Apprentice degree and sitting the Fellow Craft exam – theoretically it could be one day or one decade. In practise, however, most Freemasons will 'pass into' Fellow Craft a few weeks after being initiated as an Apprentice.

The Worshipful Master opens the lodge in a near-identical manner to the formal preambles of the Entered Apprentice degree. The sole material differences are that he asks the Deacons to ascertain that all Masons present know the Fellow Craft password, and asks the Senior Warden where he was made a Fellow Craft, being told in return:

'Within the body of a just and duly constituted lodge of Fellow Crafts, assembled in a place representing the Middle Chamber of King Solomon's Temple.'

Similarly, the waiting candidate is prepared in a manner that is sartorially similar but has certain crucial differences. Having helped the candidate to dress, the Senior Steward confirms to the meeting that he is:

'Divested of all metallic substances, neither naked nor clothed, barefoot nor shod, right knee and breast bare, hoodwinked, and with a cable-tow twice around his right arm, clothed as an Entered Apprentice.'

The candidate having knocked the door, the Senior Steward confirms to the Senior Deacon that he has *'made suitable proficiency in the preceding degree.'* The Senior Deacon demands of the Senior Steward the password of the Fellow Craft: the Senior Steward whispers it to the Senior Deacon so that the candidate cannot hear.

The Senior Deacon leads the hoodwinked candidate via the cable-tow tied twice around his right arm to the Worshipful Master. After the Worshipful Master gives permission for the degree to proceed, the Senior Deacon halts the candidate, holds an architect's square to his chest, and says:

'Brother Jones, when you first entered a Lodge of Free and Accepted Masons, you were received on the point of a sharp instrument piercing your

naked left breast, the moral of which was at the time explained to you. I am now commanded to receive you on the angle of a square applied to your naked right breast, which is to teach you that the Square of Virtue should be a rule and guide for your practice through life.'

After a brief reading by the Chaplain, the Senior Deacon circumambulates the candidate around the lodge's senior officers, telling them the password *sotto voce*, before returning him to the Worshipful Master. The Senior Warden then relays new instructions on how to *'approach the East in due and ancient form'*:

'Advance on your left foot as an Entered Apprentice. Take an additional step on your right foot, bringing the heel of your left into the hollow of your right, thereby forming the angle of a square.'

Similarly, the Worshipful Master explains the different position that the candidate must assume to receive the Obligation:

'Advance to the Sacred Altar of Freemasonry. There kneel on your naked right knee, your left forming the angle of a square, your right resting on the Volume of Sacred Law, Square and

Compasses, your left in a vertical position, your arm forming a square.'

The Fellow Craft Obligation is slightly longer than its Entered Apprentice counterpart and sees the candidate swear to honour the lodge and its orders, assist any Fellow Craft in distress and never defraud a Masonic colleague. After the cable-tow has been removed, the Worshipful Master asks the candidate, *'My Brother, in your present situation, what do you most desire?'* and is answered, *'More light in Masonry.'*

The hoodwink having been removed, the Worshipful Master tells the new Fellow Craft:

'You behold the Three Great Lights in Masonry, as in the preceding degree, with this difference: One point of the Compasses is above the Square, which is to teach you that you have received, and are entitled to receive, more Light in Masonry. But as one point is still hidden from your view, it is also to teach you that you are as yet one material point in darkness regarding Freemasonry.'

The Worshipful Master then shows the candidate the DUE-GUARD of the Fellow Craft: the heel of the left foot is placed into the hollow of the right to form the angle of a square, while the hands are again positioned as if *'my right hand is on the Volume of Sacred Law, square and compasses, my left arm is forming an angle, supported by the square, and my hand is in a vertical position'* (see illustration 5, below).

Next, he shows the candidate the SIGN of the Fellow Craft, whereby the right hand is cupped over the left breast, drawn quickly across the body and then dropped to the side, mirroring Jubelo's punishment of having *'my left breast torn open, my heart plucked out, and given to the wild beasts of the field and the fowls of the air'* (see illustration 6, below).

The Worshipful Master elicits the help of the Senior Deacon to teach the candidate the PASS-GRIP of the Fellow Craft: during a normal handshake, both men press the top of their thumb against the space between the first and second knuckle joints of the other's hand (see illustration 7, below).

WORSHIPFUL MASTER: 'Will you be off or from?'
SENIOR DEACON: 'From.'
WORSHIPFUL MASTER: 'From what and to what?'
SENIOR DEACON: 'From the grip of an Entered Apprentice to the pass-grip of a Fellow Craft.'
WORSHIPFUL MASTER: 'Pass.' [They show the pass-grip to the candidate]. 'What is that?'
SENIOR DEACON: 'The pass-grip of a Fellow Craft.'

WORSHIPFUL MASTER: 'Has it a name?'

SENIOR DEACON: 'It has.'

WORSHIPFUL MASTER: 'Will you give it to me?'

SENIOR DEACON: 'I did not so receive it; neither will I so impart it.'

WORSHIPFUL MASTER: 'How will you dispose of it?'

SENIOR DEACON: 'Letter or syllable it.'

WORSHIPFUL MASTER: 'Syllable it and begin.'

SENIOR DEACON: 'You begin.'

WORSHIPFUL MASTER: 'Begin you.'

SENIOR DEACON: 'Shib'

WORSHIPFUL MASTER: 'bo'

SENIOR DEACON: 'leth.'

The Worshipful Master then addresses the new Fellow Craft: *'Shibboleth, my Brother, is the name of this grip. You should always remember it, for should you be present at the opening of a Fellow Crafts' lodge, this pass-word will be demanded of you by one of the Deacons, and should you be unable to give it, it would cause confusion in the Craft.'*

The Worshipful Master and Senior Deacon then proceed to demonstrate the REAL GRIP of the Fellow Craft: during a standard handshake, each man presses the top of his thumb hard against the second knuckle of the other's hand (see illustration 8, below).

WORSHIPFUL MASTER: 'Will you be off or from?'
SENIOR DEACON: 'From.'
WORSHIPFUL MASTER: 'From what and to what?'
SENIOR DEACON: 'From the pass-grip of a Fellow Craft to the real grip of the same.'
WORSHIPFUL MASTER: 'Pass.' [They show the candidate]. 'What is that?'
SENIOR DEACON: 'The real grip of a Fellow Craft.'
WORSHIPFUL MASTER: 'Has it a name?'
SENIOR DEACON: 'It has.'
WORSHIPFUL MASTER: 'Will you give it to me?'
SENIOR DEACON: 'I did not so receive it; neither will I so impart it.'
WORSHIPFUL MASTER: 'How will you dispose of it?'

* * * * * * * *

Shibboleth

In ancient Hebrew, shibboleth meant either a fall of water or an ear of corn; its inclusion in the Fellow Craft degree reflects that King Solomon used to pay Fellow Craft workers on his temple in corn, amongst other goods. Ironically, in modern parlance the word means a phrase or catchword that is beloved by a sect or clique of people.

* * * * * * * *

SENIOR DEACON: 'Letter or halve it.'
WORSHIPFUL MASTER: 'Letter it and begin.'
SENIOR DEACON: 'You begin.'
WORSHIPFUL MASTER: 'Begin you.'
SENIOR DEACON: 'A.'
WORSHIPFUL MASTER: 'J.'
SENIOR DEACON: 'C.'
WORSHIPFUL MASTER: 'H.'
SENIOR DEACON: 'I.'
WORSHIPFUL MASTER: 'N.'
The Worshipful Master tells the new Fellow Craft:
'Jachin, my brother, is the name of this grip, and

should always be given in this manner, by lettering or halving it. When lettering, always commence with the letter "A".'

Having learned that the grip's name is JACHIN, again after a pillar in King Solomon's Temple, the new Fellow Craft is prompted by the Senior Deacon to demonstrate his due-guard, sign and pass-grip and real grip to the Junior and Senior Wardens.

The Senior Warden then explains how the Fellow Craft apron should be worn, and the candidate adjusts it accordingly:

'Fellow Crafts wore theirs [aprons] with the flap turned down at the lower left corner, tucked up in the form of a triangle, to serve as a receptacle for their working tools. As a Fellow Craft you will therefore wear yours in this manner, that the three sides of the triangle thus formed may symbolize the fidelity, industry and skill which should characterize your work as a Fellow Craft.'

The Worshipful Master presents the new Fellow Craft with his tool, the plumb, square and level, and explains their applications:

- the plumb was used by operative masons to ensure walls were straight and symbolizes correct, upright behaviour;

- the square was used for measuring right angles and represents honesty and being a 'square-dealing man' who is 'on the level';
- the level was used to ensure surfaces were level and symbolizes equality and justice.

The Worshipful Master then delivers a complex and highly symbolic address known as the Middle Chamber Lecture, drawing its name from the actions of King Solomon, who would sit in the Middle Chamber of his temple paying his Fellow Craft workers who had the correct password in corn, wine and oil.

The Worshipful Master describes a detailed journey that passes 'emblematically' up three flights of stairs, consisting of three, five and seven steps. Some lodges require the new Fellow Craft to walk in a circle, as if ascending a spiral staircase, as he listens to the lecture. He will also be handed corn, wine and oil.

The three steps (three is a significant number in Masonry) refer to the Three Great Lights, the three principle lodge officers, and also youth, manhood and old age. The five steps symbolize the five orders of architecture: Tuscan, Doric, Ionic, Corinthian and Composite. The final flight

* * * * * * * *

Three Precious Jewels

During the Fellow Craft degree, the Worshipful Master also presents the candidate with the Three Precious Jewels of the Attentive Ear, the Instructive Tongue and the Faithful Breast, with this instruction: 'The Attentive Ear receives the sound from the Instructive Tongue, and the mysteries of Freemasonry are safely lodged in the repository of Faithful Breasts.'

* * * * * * * *

represents the seven liberal arts and sciences: grammar, rhetoric, logic, arithmetic, geometry, music and astronomy.

When the lodge has passed emblematically into the Middle Chamber, the Worshipful Master draws their attention to the letter G suspended over his chair, explaining that it represents both geometry – the founding science of Freemasonry – and the Grand Architect of the Universe.

Having congratulated the candidate on his progress, the Worshipful Master reads the Fellow Craft Charge, urging him to speak ill of no man and to study well both Geometry and the seven liberal arts, and closes the lodge meeting in the traditional manner.

MASTER MASON DEGREE

The pinnacle of Blue Lodge Masonry, the Master Mason degree, is said to be the 'supreme and exalted rank' of Freemasonry and is consequently longer and more complex than its predecessors – as well as featuring a role-playing climax absent from both the Entered Apprentice and Fellow Craft exams.

The Worshipful Master opens the lodge for the Master Mason degree in the by-now familiar fashion. The only diversion from routine is an intriguing section of early dialogue that achieves significance later in the ceremony:

WORSHIPFUL MASTER: 'Have you ever travelled as a Master Mason?'

SENIOR WARDEN: 'I have, from West to East, and from East to West again.'

WORSHIPFUL MASTER: 'Of what were you in search?'

* * * * * * * *

The Third Degree

The examination and catechisms of third-degree Masonry are considered so onerous that they gave rise to the common expression 'Given the third degree', meaning being subjected to lengthy and sustained bouts of difficult questioning.

* * * * * * * *

SENIOR WARDEN: 'Of that which was lost.'

WORSHIPFUL MASTER: 'To what do you allude?'

SENIOR WARDEN: 'The secret word of a Master Mason.'

WORSHIPFUL MASTER: 'Did you find it?'

SENIOR WARDEN: 'I did not, but I found a substitute.'

The formalities being completed, the candidate is admitted to the lodge, once it is ascertained he has satisfied the – once again – very specific dress code: *'Divested of all metallic substances, neither naked nor clothed, barefoot, both knees and breasts bare, hoodwinked and with a cable-tow three times around his body, clothed as a Fellow Craft.'*

The Senior Steward whispers the secret password to the Senior Deacon, who leads the candidate to the Worshipful Master for his approval. Having secured it, the Senior Deacon presses an opened compass to the chest of the hoodwinked man, explaining: *'I am now commanded to receive you on the extreme points of the compasses, extending from your naked right to your naked left breast, which is to teach you that as within the breast are contained the most vital parts of man, so between the extreme points of the compasses are contained the most valuable tenets of Freemasonry, which are Friendship, Morality and Brotherly Love.'*

After the chaplain's reading, the Senior Deacon again circumambulates the candidate around the lodge whispering the password to the Wardens before returning to the Worshipful Master, who orders the Senior Warden to tell the candidate how to approach the East. He does so: *'Brother Jones, advance on your left foot as an Entered Apprentice, and on your right as a Fellow Craft. Take an additional step on your left foot, bringing the heel of your right to the heel of your left, thereby forming the angle of a square.'*

* * * * * * * *

Going Slipshod

**The candidate for the first two degrees comes 'slipshod'
i.e. wearing one loose slipper but with one foot bare.
The candidate for the Master Mason ceremony is fully
barefoot as during the ritual he will emblematically enter
the holiest of holy places – the Sanctum Sanctorum of
King Solomon's Temple.**

* * * * * * * *

The Worshipful Master instructs the Mason to
adopt the position to receive the Obligation of the
Master Mason: *'Advance to the Sacred Altar of
Freemasonry. There kneel on your naked knees, both
hands resting on the Volume of Sacred Law, Square
and Compasses.'*

This Obligation is a lengthy catechism wherein
the candidate vows never to commit a volley of
Masonic taboos, including inappropriately using
secret words or signs, attacking fellow Masons
and having carnal intercourse with their wives.
Once his cable-tow and hoodwink have been taken
off, the Worshipful Master informs him: *'My*

Brother, on being brought to light in this degree, you behold the Three Great Lights of Masonry as in the preceding degree, with this difference: both points of the Compasses are above the Square, which is to teach you that you have received and are entitled to receive all the Light than can be conferred upon or communicated to you in a Master Masons' lodge.'

The Worshipful Master shows the candidate the DUE-GUARD of the Master Mason: the heel of the right foot is brought to the heel of the left to form the angle of a square, while the hands are placed as if *'both hands are resting on the Holy Bible, Squares and Compasses'* (see illustration 9, p. 182).

Next, he shows the candidate the SIGN of the Master Mason, whereby the thumb of the right hand is drawn quickly across the waist to the right hip, then dropped to the side, symbolizing Jubelum's punishment of having *'my body cut in two, my bowels removed and burned to ashes which are then scattered to the four winds of Heaven'* (see illustration 10, p. 183, top).

As usual, the Worshipful Master calls upon the Senior Deacon to help him demonstrate the PASS-GRIP of the Master Mason: during a normal handshake, both men press their thumbs

hard between the second and third knuckles of
the other's hand (see illustration 11, right, bottom).
Their call-and-response dialogue then follows its
normal pattern until this point:

WORSHIPFUL MASTER: 'How will you dispose
of it?'

SENIOR DEACON: 'Letter or syllable it.'

* * * * * * * *

Tubalcain

Genesis 4: 18 describes Lamech, a great-great-great-grandson of Adam and Eve's son, Cain. Lamech had two wives, Adah and Zillah, by whom he had three sons – Jabell, Juball and Tubal – and a daughter, Mahmah. Masonic legend claims that these four children 'found the beginning of all the crafts in the world'. Interestingly, while Jabell invented geometry and built the first house of stone and timber, and would have been a more appropriate Masonic icon, Tubal was 'an instructor of every artificer in brass and iron' (Genesis 4: 22).

* * * * * * * *

WORSHIPFUL MASTER: 'Syllable it and begin.'
SENIOR DEACON: 'You begin.'
WORSHIPFUL MASTER: 'Begin you.'
SENIOR DEACON: 'Tu'
WORSHIPFUL MASTER: 'bal'
SENIOR DEACON: 'cain.'
The Senior Deacon prompts the candidate to show the due-guard, sign and pass-grip to the Junior

and Senior Warden, before the Senior Warden instructs the new Master Mason how he should henceforth wear his apron: *'Master Masons wore theirs turned down in the form of a square to designate them as Master Masons or overseers of the work. As a speculative Master Mason you will therefore wear yours in this manner, to admonish you that your acts towards all mankind should possess the qualities of that perfect figure; to symbolise the integrity of your service to God, and to remind you of the four-fold duty; to your country, your neighbour, your family and yourself.'*

The Worshipful Master then gives him the tools of the Master Mason's trade, which vary between different Masonic jurisdictions. Some lodges award a skirret, pencil and compass:

- the skirret (a pin and marker used to draw straight lines) symbolizes the necessity of 'straight-down-the-line' moral behaviour;
- the pencil reminds the Mason that all of his conduct is noted;
- the compass maps out parameters and stands for good judgement.

However, at many lodges the Worshipful Master emblematically presents the candidate with: '... *all the tools in Masonry but especially the Trowel. The Trowel is an instrument used by operative Masons to spread the cement which unites the building into one common mass: but we, as Free and Accepted Masons, are taught to use it for the more noble and glorious purpose of spreading the cement of brotherly love and affection.'*

At this point the lodge rises for either a short break or possibly a Festive Board, before returning for the second half of the Master Mason degree – a dramatic re-enactment of the murder at King Solomon's Temple of Hiram Abiff.

For this striking section of the ceremony, the candidate plays the central role of the slain architect, while the Worshipful Grand Master takes the part of King Solomon and the Senior Warden is Hiram, King of Tyre, the symbolic 'Senior Warden' of Solomon's Temple. The other parts are read by Master Masons from the lodge.

When the lodge reconvenes, the candidate is sitting in the Junior Warden's seat and wearing his jewel of office. The Worshipful Master asks him the time and, receiving no answer, asks again: 'Brother Junior Warden, what is the time?'

SENIOR WARDEN: 'Worshipful Master, there appears to be a stranger in the South.'

WORSHIPFUL MASTER: 'What? A stranger in the South! Brother Senior Deacon, conduct the stranger to the East.'

The Worshipful Master explains to the candidate that he has not yet achieved the 'sublime degree of Master Mason' and to do so he must undertake a perilous journey that may result in his death *as did once befall an eminent Brother of this degree'*. The candidate kneels at the altar to pray for divine assistance: while he does so, he is again hoodwinked.

The candidate now represents Hiram Abiff but says nothing during the drama that ensues, being required only to physically act out the events that are narrated. The Senior Deacon sets the scene: *'It was the usual custom of this great and good man, at high twelve, when the Craft was called from labour to refreshment, to enter the Sanctum Sanctorum, or Holy of Holies, there to order up his adorations to Deity and draw his designs on the Trestle-board. This you have done. He would then retire by the South gate, as you do now.'*

Moving to the south of the lodge room, the

* * * * * * * *

The Fatal Maul

Jubelum murders Hiram Abiff with a maul, or gavel, a small heavy mallet used by stonemasons to hammer finished stones firmly in place while building walls. The most brutally effective and least subtle of tools, it stands symbolically for acts of violence and destruction.

* * * * * * * *

candidate is confronted by a Mason representing Jubela, the 'First Ruffian', who demands of him the secrets of a Master Mason. Refusing him, Hiram Abiff flees to the west side of the lodge where another Mason, playing Jubelo, makes the same request, threatening him: *'Grand Master Hiram, your life is in danger. All the avenues of the Temple are securely guarded; escape is impossible. I therefore demand of you the secrets of a Master Mason.'*

The candidate then runs to the east side of the lodge, where Jubelum stops him and warns that he has in his hand *'an instrument of death'* and will kill him if he does not yield the information. Retorting

* * * * * * * *

The Helpful Sailor

One character in the Master Mason degree killing of Hiram Abiff is a 'Sea-Faring Man'. Asked for passage to Ethiopia by Jubela, Jubelo and Jubelum after they have slain the architect, he refuses because they do not have the necessary permission to leave the country signed by King Solomon. He later points the murderers' pursuers on their trail towards their quarry.

* * * * * * * *

that his demands are 'vain', Hiram Abiff refuses three times: after the third time, Jubelum strikes him on the forehead with a maul.

The candidate falls backwards into a large canvas held by Masons. The three ruffians immediately repent of the killing, with Jubelum declaring: *'Kept to well, his secret stands revealed, and in his death I read it thus: Truth – Honour – Fortitude'.* Nevertheless, they carry Hiram in the canvas to a corner of the lodge and 'bury' him, placing a sprig of acacia by the grave, before fleeing.

Twelve Fellow Crafts 'clothed in white gloves

and aprons' then approach King Solomon, played by the Worshipful Master. Confessing that they were part of the plan to kill Hiram Abiff but dropped out, they are dispatched by Solomon to find and capture Jubela, Jubelo and Jubelum.

One search party overhears the three ruffians bemoaning their crime, captures them and returns to Solomon, who orders them put to death. The King then commands the other plotters to locate Hiram Abiff's body and *'observe whether the Master's Word, or a key to it, is on or about it.'*

These Masons discover the sprig of acacia and gather around the prone candidate but are horrified at the state of decay of Hiram Abiff's corpse: *'Here is a body, but in such a mangled and putrid condition that it cannot be recognised. What a deadly effluvium arises from it!'*

Finding no Master's Word or key to it on the candidate's body, they instead take Hiram Abiff's jewel to King Solomon to confirm his identity. Solomon then instructs the Craft to follow him in *'Grand Procession'*: *'... to endeavour to raise the body of our Grand Master Hiram Abiff for more decent internment; and as the Master's Word is now lost, it is my order that the first sign given at the grave, and the first word spoken after the body is raised, shall be adopted for the regulation of all Masters Lodges, until future ages shall find out the right.'*

The entire lodge then form the Grand Procession behind the Worshipful Master, singing a dirge as they go:

Solemn strikes the funeral chime
Notes of our departing time;
As we journey here below
Through a pilgrimage of woe.
Mortals now indulge a tear
For mortality is here.
See how wide her trophies wave
O'er the slumbers of the grave.
Here another guest we bring.
Seraphs of celestial wing,
To our funeral altar come:
Waft this friend and brother home.
There, enlarged, thy soul shall see
What was veiled in mystery;
Heavenly glories of the place
Show his Maker, face to face.
Lord of all, below – above
Fill our hearts with truth and love.

> *When dissolves our earthly tie,*
> *Take us to thy Lodge on High.*

The Craft gather around the candidate and the Worshipful Master orders the Senior Warden to lift the body of Hiram Abiff using the grip of the Entered Apprentice. The Senior Warden tries to do so but offers the grisly report that *'owing to the high state of putrefaction, the body having been dead fifteen days, the skin slips from the flesh and it can not so be raised.'* The whole lodge then raise their arms, forming a square at the elbow, and cry *'Is there no help for the Widow's Son?'*

The Worshipful Master commands the Senior Warden to try again using the grip of the Fellow Craft, but again *'the flesh cleaves from the bone'* and the attempt fails. The lodge then twice repeat the Widow's Son imprecation and the chaplain says a prayer, before King Solomon addresses the Craft: *'The Master's Word is lost in the death of your Grand Master Hiram Abiff but I will substitute a word ... Yea, my Brethren, I have a Word; and though the skin may slip from the flesh, and the flesh cleaves from the bones, there is strength in the Lion of the Tribe of Judah, and he shall prevail.'*

* * * * * * * *

Quiet as The Grave

Some Masonic lodges have a hollow built into the ground purely for the purpose of serving as a grave for Hiram Abiff. Others use actual coffins, although this practice has largely died out.

It has been argued that there is a resurrection element to this section of the third degree, possibly mirroring the Egyptian myth of Osiris who came back from the dead, but Freemasonry does not claim that Hiram Abiff was resurrected, merely that his body was removed from its temporary grave.

* * * * * * * *

King Solomon then reaches down and grasps Hiram Abiff's hand in the real grip of a Master Mason: the two Masons interlace their thumbs and press their fingers, which are slightly apart, against the inner wrist of the other man's hand (see illustration 12, page 194).

The Worshipful Master then raises the candidate from the ground using the technique known

* * * * * * * *

The Lion of Judah

The Lion of Judah traditionally symbolized the royal tribe of the Hebrew nation, with each King becoming the Lion. This would therefore have been one of King Solomon's many honorary titles.

* * * * * * * *

as the Five Points of Fellowship (see illustration 13, opposite). As he does so, he whispers the substitute word into his ear: *'Ma-ha-bone'*.

Worshipful Master: *'My Brother, the word you have just received is a Hebrew word and signifies 'What? The Builder?'* It alludes to a particular tie in your Obligation wherein you swore that you would

never give the substitute for the Master's Word in any other way or manner than that in which you would receive it, which would be on the Five Points of Fellowship and at low breath.

'The Five Points of Fellowship are: foot to foot; knee to knee; breast to breast; hand to back; and cheek to cheek or mouth to ear. And teach us these important lessons:

- *Foot to foot, that we should be ever ready to go on foot, even barefoot, on a worthy Master Mason's errand, should his necessities require it, and we be no better provided.*
- *Knee to knee, that we should ever remember our Brethren in our devotion to Deity.*
- *Breast to breast, that the secrets of a worthy Brother Master Mason, when communicated to us as such, should be as secure and inviolate in our breasts as they were in his before communication.*
- *Hand to back, that we should be ever ready to stretch forth a hand to support a falling Brother, and aid him on all lawful occasions.*
- *Cheek to cheek, or mouth to ear, that we should be ever ready to whisper wise counsel in the ear of an erring Brother, and warn him of approaching danger.'*

At the end of this oration, the Worshipful Master elicits the help of the Senior Deacon to formally teach the candidate the real grip of the Master Mason. The Worshipful Master and candidate then arrange themselves on the Five Points of Fellowship to exchange the Word (or, rather, substitute Word) of the Master Mason: Worshipful Master: *'Ma'*

Candidate: *'ha'*

Worshipful Master: *'bone'*.

The Worshipful Master then teaches the candidate the Grand Hailing Sign of Distress of a Master Mason: as previously, both arms are raised skywards, forming a square at the elbows, then lowered to the sides in three distinct motions (see illustration 14, page 198). He explains that if a Master Mason is in distress in a place where the Sign cannot be given, he may substitute the words *'Is there no help for the Widow's Son?'* with *'the Sign and the words are never to be given together'*.

The degree ceremony concludes with the Master Mason's lecture. Delivered by a lodge officer, it recaps the story of the building of King Solomon's Temple and the murder of Hiram Abiff before explaining delving into the symbolism behind a host of Masonic emblems.

The Worshipful Master reads the Master Mason Charges to the now fully qualified Master Mason, bidding him to be exemplary in his conduct and a mentor to less-qualified Masons. He may then be asked to sign a declaration at the lodge Secretary's desk, after which the meeting is closed.

Appendant Degrees

Around three-quarters of British Freemasons take no further degrees beyond the Master Mason degree of the Blue Lodge. However, further appendant degrees are hugely popular in America and, to a lesser degree, France. It is not the purpose of this book to detail these auxiliary qualifications too closely, but they are worthy of cursory investigation.

The two leading Masonic appendant bodies are the York Rite and Scottish Rite and both provide an opportunity for Freemasons to continue their moral and historical studies. It is stressed, however, that no qualification is more important than, or superior to, the Blue Lodge Master Mason degree.

The York Rite

The York Rite takes its name from the Regius Manuscript of 1390, which describes King Athelstan convening the first Grand Lodge of Masons in York in 926 AD. It also has historical links to the breakaway 1725 Grand Lodge of All England at York, which conferred more degrees than the three Blue Lodge qualifications awarded by the Grand Lodge of England.

Largely popular in America, the York Rite is a term covering three separate Masonic bodies which confer a total of ten additional degrees: four Royal Arch degrees, three Cryptic Mason degrees and three Chivalric Orders.

Royal Arch Masonry

Royal Arch Masonry meetings in America are held in local Chapters that are governed by Grand Chapters in a close approximation of the traditional lodge structure. The officer structure is different, with members awarded such high-flown titles as High Priest, King and Grand Master of the Third Veil. The Royal Arch confers four Masonic degrees, of which the fourth – the Royal Arch degree – is by far the most significant.

MARK MASTER

The first York Rite degree is known as the fourth degree as it follows on from the standard Blue Lodge degrees – only Master Masons are allowed to study the York or Scottish Rites. The Mark Master degree dates from operative stonemasons traditionally carving their own individual marks into the edifices they were working on.

Past Master

Also known as the Virtual Past Master degree, this qualification was first introduced in America to circumvent a previous ruling that only former Blue Lodge Worshipful Past Masters could study Royal Arch Masonry. A *Coles Notes* version of Worshipful Master learning, it is ignored in England.

Most Excellent Master

One of the most flamboyant rituals in Freemasonry, the Most Excellent Master degree describes the completion of the construction of King Solomon's Temple. Invented in America in the late 1700s, it forms part of the Cryptic Rite within English Masonry.

Royal Arch

The extraordinary Royal Arch degree describes the discovery of a crypt beneath King Solomon's Temple after the Temple was demolished and details the spiritual treasures supposedly found within it. It also, crucially, reveals the Master Mason's Word that the third Blue Lodge degree claims was lost with the murder of Hiram Abiff.

The three senior chapter officers (known as Principles) conduct the Royal Arch degree, including the following catechism: First Officer: *'In the beginning was the Word.'*

Second Officer: *'And the Word was with God.'*

Third Officer: *'And the Word was God.'*

After this recitation – the opening verse of the Gospel of St John – the First Principle asks *'Companions, Principles, what are the great attributes of these mysterious words?'* and is told: *'Omniscience'.*

'Omnipotence'.

'Omnipresence'.

The chapter room is then slightly transformed to emblematically assume the appearance of a rebuilt King Solomon's Temple, and two of the Principles question and answer each other: *'Why did you leave Babylon to go to Jerusalem?'*

'To assist in rebuilding the second Temple, and to endeavour to obtain the sacred word.'

The three Principles then form a human triangle, each holding the right wrist of the Principle on his left and the left wrist of the Principle on his right, thereby forming two triangles interlaced into a Seal of Solomon. Forming a further triangle with their feet, they recite in unison:

'As we three agree
In peace, love and unity
The sacred word to keep
So we three do agree
In peace, love and unity
The sacred word to search.
Until we three,
Or three such as we shall agree
This Royal Arch Chapter to close.'

The three Principles then whisper the sacred word three times to the candidate, each saying one syllable: *'Jah' 'Bul' 'On'.*

'Jah' 'Bul' 'On'.
'Jah' 'Bul' 'On'.

A Principle tells the candidate: *'It is the name of the Deity in three languages, viz Chaldee, Hebrew and Syriac, which is the long lost Master Mason's Word, and has now become the Grand Omnific Royal Arch Word.'*

* * * * * * * *

Jahbulon

The Masonic 'Lost Word' Jahbulon is a compound of three gods: Jehovah, or Jahweh, the Hebrew God, the Semitic deity Baal, and Osiris the Egyptian God (whose followers would chant 'On' to call upon him). Even the secret ritual book of Royal Arch Masonry does not print the Lost Word in full, referring to it instead by the initials J.B.O.

* * * * * * * *

The Principles elucidate further: *'[Jahbulon is] the names by which the Supreme Being was known to the three leading nations of antiquity – Chaldean, Syrian and Egyptian:*

- *Jah – the Chaldean name of God, and signifies "His essence in Majesty – incomprehensible". It is also a Hebrew word, signifying "I am and shall be", thereby expressing the actual future and eternal existence of the Most High.*
- *Bal is a Syriac word which signifies "Lord or Powerful" and also "Lord in Heaven or on high".*

- *On is an Egyptian word signifying "Father of all" as it is expressed in the Lord's Prayer.'*

A Principle describes a search of the crypt beneath Solomon's Temple, and what lies beneath the first arch: *'The discovery you have made is of the greatest importance. It is no less than the long-lost book of the holy law. You see now that the world is indebted to Freemasonry for the preservation of this sacred volume. Had it not been for the Masonic wisdom and precaution of our Grand Master, this only remaining copy of the law would have been lost at the destruction of the Temple.'*

The 'Grand Master' referred to is Hiram Abiff, who purportedly hid the book of Solomon's teachings under the arch – doubtless it was stored next to the 'Sangreal documents' of Dan Brown's *The Da Vinci Code*. As the degree continues, the Principle emblematically gives the new Royal Arch Mason a copy of this book bearing the Latin legend *'Nil nisi lavis deest'*: 'Only the key is wanting.'

The Principles search symbolically under the second arch of the crypt but find nothing. Under the third arch, however, they locate Freemasonry's Holy Grail, Dan Brown's Solomon Key itself: *'We*

* * * * * * * *

Only The Key is Wanting

Fundamentalist Christians find faults with Freemasonry on copious levels, but most are centred on the Royal Arch degree. Evangelists regard the 'corruption' of Jehovah or Jahweh in the word Jahbulon as blasphemous, as is the idea that a Kabbalah-esque code – or Solomon Key – is required fully to understand the Bible.

* * * * * * * *

discovered a key-stone of a third arch: on removing it, the sun, having now gained its meridian height, darted its rays to the centre. It shone resplendent on a white marble pedestal, whereon was a plate of gold. On this plate was engraved a triple triangle, and within the triangle some characters which are beyond comprehension.'

This plate contains bears the word Jahbulon, *'three mysterious words, in a triangle form, the long-lost sacred word of the Master Mason, and too incomprehensible for individual expression'.* The Principles stress that no Mason can say the Word

* * * * * * * *

The Missing Link?

The Royal Arch degree is effectively the second half of the Master Mason degree, wherein the missing Master's Word is rediscovered. The Antients vs Moderns Masonic schism of the late 1700s was largely predicated on this topic and some English lodges still confer the Royal Arch degree.

* * * * * * * *

in its entirety, only syllable it in whispers. Having presented the candidate with a purple and crimson Royal Arch Mason sash and apron, they close the Chapter.

Cryptic Masonry

Conferred by the Council of Royal and Select Masters, the Cryptic Rite contains three degrees, again based on the contents of the fabled crypt beneath King Solomon's Temple.

ROYAL MASTER

The Royal Master degree uses the imagery of a Fellow Craft questing for knowledge. Although it describes a time before the building of Solomon's Temple, Hiram Abiff is again central.

SELECT MASTER

The Select Master ritual stresses Masonry's moral compass, and explains how the secrets of the Temple were hidden in its crypt before the first edifice was demolished.

SUPER EXCELLENT MASTER

This ambitiously titled ceremony describes the mistakes made by Solomon's successors that led to the Exodus of the Jews from Jerusalem. (Some US Chapters award a fourth Cryptic Rite degree: the Thrice Universal Master).

Chivalric Masonry

The three final degrees of the York Rite are awarded by the Commandery of Knights Templar, and are unique amongst Masonic degrees in being specifically Christian in nature: candidates are asked to swear faith in the Holy Trinity of the Father, Son and Holy Ghost.

The Worshipful Master figure in a Knights Templar Commandery is called an Eminent Commander and the US controlling body is the Grand Encampment. However, the Commandery claims no historical lineage from the warrior knights, so there are slim pickings for Dan Brown here.

ILLUSTRIOUS ORDER OF THE RED CROSS

The first Chivalric degree portrays Prince Zerubbabel asking permission to rebuild King Solomon's Temple circa 520 BC. It is peculiar to the US York Rite and is not awarded in England or Scotland.

ORDER OF MALTA

Based around the iconography of the Maltese Cross, this flamboyant ritual confers both the Mediterranean Pass and the Order of Malta and depicts a crusading knight temporarily billeted on Malta. The successful candidate becomes a Knight Hospitaller – historically, a fellow order of the Knights Templar.

ORDER OF THE TEMPLE

The Valiant and Magnanimous Order of the Temple re-enacts a medieval monk's initiation into the Knights Templar and includes poetic references to the Christ story. When the plucky Freemason has completed this degree, he can describe himself as a Knight Templar.

Scottish Rite

Originally fabricated by the fertile imagination of Paris-dwelling Scottish Mason Andrew Michael Ramsay, who claimed in 1737 that Freemasons were directly descended from the Knights Templar, the Scottish Rite was formalized by notorious Masonic scholar Albert Pike in his 1868 tract *Morals and Dogma*. It is, again, a largely American phenomenon.

Today, the Scottish Rite is overseen by Supreme Councils who regulate the activities of local lodge/Chapter-like groups named valleys. It awards thirty-two degrees (including the Blue Lodge degrees) plus the mysterious 33rd degree, which is awarded only to selected individuals and

* * * * * * * *

Only in America

The large-scale, epic-effect 'McMasons' Scottish Rite degree ceremonies are unique to the US and frowned upon by more traditionalist Freemasons. Other nations where the Scottish Rite is prevalent, such as France, tend to do things rather more intimately.

* * * * * * * *

is a constant source of fascination to conspiracy theorists – of this, more anon.

Unlike Blue Lodge and York Rite degrees, Scottish Rite ceremonies in the US take place in grand, theatre-like halls with dramatic scenery, costumes and lighting. One candidate plays the central role in the onstage production on behalf of scores of others, watching in the audience, who rise en masse to give signs or recite Obligations as appropriate.

The 33 degrees of the Scottish Rite are sectioned into four *divisions*, or ranks, but these vary in the US between the valleys administered by the Southern Masonic Jurisdiction (SMJ) and the

Northern Masonic Jurisdiction (NMJ). The SMJ remains more true to the rituals clarified by pioneering Arkansas Freemason Albert Pike, so we shall focus on these while nodding briefly towards NMJ variations at the end.

Lodge Of Perfection

SMJ Masonry calls Scottish Rite degrees numbers 4–14 (degrees 1–3 are, again, the standard Blue Lodge qualifications) the Lodge of Perfection. Functioning as moral fables to further Masonic education, these rituals are sometimes called the Ineffable Degrees and tell the story of the Hiramic Legend via dramatic re-enactments of the following events:

4) SECRET MASTER – King Solomon appoints seven Masons to guard the *Sanctum Sanctorum*.

5) PERFECT MASTER – the killing of Hiram Abiff.

6) INTIMATE SECRETARY – Solomon protects a Mason accused of treachery.

7) PROVOST AND JUDGE – the murder trial of Hiram Abiff 's killers.

* * * * * * * *

Tetragrammaton

The Grand Elect Perfect and Sublime degree culminates in the discovery of the Tetragrammaton on the Pillar of Beauty in Solomon's crypt. Comprising four Hebrew letters – Yod, He, Waw and He – the Tetragrammaton is said to be the four-letter name of God, pronounced Jehovah or Yahweh (see illustration 15, below).

יהוה

* * * * * * * *

8) INTENDANT OF THE BUILDING – the Temple is finished after Hiram Abiff's death.
9) ELU (or election) OF THE NINE.
10) ELU OF THE FIFTEEN.
11) ELU OF THE TWELVE – these three degrees are concerned with the Masons given the task of judging and sentencing Hiram Abiff's killers.
12) GRAND MASTER ARCHITECT – how ancient master builders learnt their trade.

213

13) ROYAL ARCH OF SOLOMON (Knight of the
Ninth Arch).

14) GRAND ELECT PERFECT AND SUBLIME
MASON – these two degrees take place in the
crypt beneath Solomon's Temple: once they are
completed the Mason is said to be himself a
potential corporeal Lodge of Perfection.

Chapter of Rose Croix

The SMJ's Scottish Rite degrees 15–18 are known
as the Chapter of the Rose Croix and deal thema-
tically with the rebuilding of King Solomon's
Temple by Zerubbabel. These ceremonies are
alternatively known as the Capitular Degrees.

15) KNIGHT OF THE EAST (or the Sword of the
Eagle) – Jewish captives in Babylon return to
Jerusalem to rebuild the Temple.

16) PRINCE OF JERUSALEM – the hardships of
building the second Temple.

17) KNIGHT OF THE EAST AND WEST – Jerusalem
as a bridge between Heaven and Earth.

18) KNIGHT OF THE ROSE CROIX – expressly
Christian in content, the last of the Capitular

* * * * * * * *

Masons and the Rose Cross (Croix)

It is tempting to draw a direct correlation between the Scottish Rite's Chapter of the Rose Cross and the seventeenth century Rosicrucian movement founded by the fictitious Christian Rosenkreutz. This is feasible, but it should be noted that the Rose and Cross, standing for a meeting of the divine and human worlds, has been an esoteric symbol since ancient times.

* * * * * * * *

Degrees references both Maundy Thursday and Easter Sunday and can be regarded as a Masonic take on the Passion of the Christ.

Council of Kadosh

Degrees 19–30 of the SMJ-administered Scottish Rite are known as the Council of Kadosh. Kadosh is a Hebrew word meaning 'holy' or 'sacred'. The first 11 of the 12 are also called the Degrees of Areopagus. These rituals are chivalric, abstracted

* * * * * * * *

Kabbalah

Some esoteric scholars have linked speculative Freemasonry with Kabbalah, the opaque mystical Jewish discipline of Biblical interpretation. There are certain similarities in the applications of codes and keys in search of a moral and spiritual Greater Truth, and elements of the Council of Kadosh degrees are distinctly Kabbalistic.

* * * * * * * *

and contain mystical material, emphasizing the following qualities that should always be culti-vated by Freemasons:

19) GRAND PONTIFF – constant self-improvement.

20) MASTER OF THE SYMBOLIC LODGE – liberty, fraternity and equality.

21) NOACHITE (or Prussian Knight) – upright behaviour.

22) KNIGHT OF THE ROYAL AXE, PRINCE OF LIBANUS – hard and diligent work (Libanus is an ancient name for Lebanon, from where

Hiram, Prince of Tyre supplied cedar for King Solomon's Temple).

23) CHIEF OF THE TABERNACLE – divine faith.

24) PRINCE OF THE TABERNACLE – compassion and fellowship.

25) KNIGHT OF THE BRAZEN SERPENT – overcoming despair.

26) PRINCE OF MERCY (or Scottish Trinitarian) – wisdom and forgiveness.

27) KNIGHT OF THE SUN (or Prince Adept) – truth and reason.

28) KNIGHT COMMANDER OF THE TEMPLE – chivalry (based around Crusader warriors the Teutonic Knights).

29) SCOTTISH KNIGHT OF ST ANDREW – tolerance and understanding.

30) KNIGHT KADOSH – emphasizing the ongoing quest for personal spiritual perfection, it is also known as the Degree Kadosh.

Consistory Degrees

The two Consistory Degrees represent the culmination of the teachings of the Scottish Rite and outline the ideal spiritual balance a Freemason should attain between spiritual awareness and physical reality.

31) INSPECTOR INQUISITOR - this judicial explains the need for constant moral self-examination

32) MASTER OF THE ROYAL SECRET - a military-based degree emphasizing the role of sacrifice.

NOTES

1) The US Northern Masonic Jurisdiction, covering the Northern states and Canada, divides its Scottish Rite very differently. The NMJ calls rituals 15 and 16 the Council Princes of Jerusalem degrees and regards ceremonies 19–32 as Consistory Degrees.

2) NMJ degrees 20, 25 and 26 also veer spectacularly from the SMJ template and involve considerations of the characters and historical achievements of US icons George Washington, Benjamin Franklin and Abraham Lincoln.

3) Degrees 27 and 28 were reversed in a large-scale revision of the SMJ Scottish Rite ceremonies between 1995 and 2000.

The 33rd degree

33) INSPECTOR GENERAL

The 33rd degree of the Scottish Rite is awarded by the Supreme Council for exceptional contributions to Freemasonry or public life. It is conferred by invitation only and – theoretically at least – cannot be requested or lobbied for.

Candidates for Inspector General must already be 32nd degree Masons and must be at least thirty-three years old, and the Supreme Council will only select thirty-three 33rd degree Masons from any region at any time. Freemasons who are so honoured are referred to as Illustrious 33rds and may write 33 after their name on Masonic papers.

Dan Brown is not the only conspiracy theorist, whether disingenuous or earnest, to make hay with the notion of a 'secret' sinister 33rd Masonic degree. In their late nineties tract *The Brotherhood and the Manipulation of Society*, anti-Masonic writers Ivan Fraser and Mark Beeston argued that 33 degree Freemasons clandestinely occupy top positions in government, police, the judiciary and the global military-industrial complex:

'*At the apex of the pyramid of the Brotherhood are the select few who actually know the full agenda of the organization. These privileged few have become known as the Illuminati ... all other members (nearly five million worldwide) are ignorant of the true purposes of their individual organization as a front for the Illuminati. Only the most suitable are selected to rise in the ranks, those recognized as being wealthy, ambitious and corrupt enough to perpetuate the ultimate goal, which is world domination.*'

Fraser and Beeston's view of Freemasonry as the modern incarnation of secret controlling esoteric sects such as the Knights Templar and Knights of Malta is entertaining froth but hardly chimes with the reality of proudly grinning septuagenarian Masons sporting absurdly decorated aprons. In Freemasonry terms, being conferred as a 33 degree is rather more akin to being awarded the key to the executive washroom.

– 4 –

MASONIC SYMBOLS –
A BRIEF GUIDE

In line with its self-description as 'a peculiar system of morality, veiled in allegory and illuminated by symbols', Freemasonry is awash with symbols. In addition to the emblems already discussed in descriptions of Masonry's rituals, copious objects about the lodge, ideas and even phrases are charged with deeper symbolic import. Some associations are directly derived from operative stonemasons, while others are infinitely more abstract and tenuous – but the following are all items that resound with profound significance within Masonic thinking.

24-INCH GAUGE
A ruler split into three sections to represent a life well lived – eight hours per day devoted to work, eight to good deeds, and eight to sleep.

3

The number 3 is significant in Masonry, from the three Blue Lodge degrees, chief lodge officers, candles on the altar and steps leading to the chair of the Worshipful Master to the three Royal Arch Principles who form a triangle to whisper 'Jahbulon – the name of the Deity in three languages.'

47TH PROPOSITION OF EUCLID

A jewel sometimes awarded to lodge Past Masters, it represents the most significant equation in architecture: Pythagoras's Theorem that in an equilateral triangle, the sum of the hypotenuse is equal to the sum of the square of the other two sides.

ACACIA

Placed at the grave of Hiram Abiff by his penitent killers, acacia is a sturdy evergreen plant representing survival and rebirth.

ALL-SEEING EYE

This fabled symbol is not Masonic in origin but is often used in lodges as a deistic, non-denominational representation of the Great Architect of the Universe.

ANCHOR AND THE ARK
Biblical imagery representing grounding and safe passage through the turbulent sea of troubles of everyday life.

ASHLARS
A rough ashlar (building stone) symbolizes man in ignorance, while a smooth ashlar suggests wisdom and sophistication.

BEEHIVE
Used in the Blue Lodge Master Mason's degree to illustrate the dual ideas of productive labour and geometric precision.

CABLE-TOW
Worn by Masons during degree ceremonies to indicate willingness to be led towards knowledge.

Chalk, charcoal and clay
An element of the Entered Apprentice degree ritual, these rudimentary materials represent willingness to serve at a lowly level.

Circumambulation
Walking around a lodge from East to West via South to mirror the trajectory of the sun.

Coffin and Spade
These two items are both inexorably linked in Masonic thinking with the murder of Hiram Abiff.

Compass
Used in geometry and architecture and represents restraint, skill and knowledge – a compass maps out the emblematic perfect circle whose borders proscribe a Mason's behaviour.

Corn, wine and oil
Awarded to a candidate during the Fellow Craft degree, these items of natural produce symbolize the wages paid to craftsmen labouring on King Solomon's Temple – and also a tithe that Solomon paid to Hiram, King of Tyre in exchange for his

help in building it. Corn symbolizes abundance, wine stands for good health and oil represents contentment.

Cornucopia

The cornucopia, or horn of plenty, is the jewel of office of lodge senior and junior wardens, and signifies that they are responsible for providing the food and drink for Masonic festive boards.

Double-headed eagle

This startlingly dramatic image is the US symbol for the Scottish Rite. The eagle's wings normally point down but some 33 degree Masons are allowed to have the wings pointing up.

Five-pointed star

Represents both the divine and the Five Points of Fellowship stance used to raise Hiram Abiff from the grave in the Master Mason's degree.

G

Suspended over the Worshipful Master's chair at the East of the lodge, it symbolizes the Great Architect of the Universe and geometry.

GAVEL

This stone hammer is emblematically used to hew away the rough edges from a Mason's character and behaviour.

HEART AND SWORD

This emblem from the Master Mason's degree symbolizes the fact that God, or the Great Architect of the Universe, is always watching Man and will reward or punish his deeds.

HOODWINK

The blindfold worn during degree rituals to indicate moral darkness and ignorance, but removed to receive the light of Masonic knowledge.

HOURGLASS

The hourglass appears during the Master Mason degree to signify intimations of mortality and the inevitable passing of the sands of time.

INDENTED TASSEL

These tassels attached to a cord around the outside of the tracing board for the Entered Apprentice degree represent Masonry's four cardinal virtues of temperance, fortitude, prudence and justice.

JACOB'S LADDER

Linked to the winding staircase of the Fellow Craft degree, Masonry regards the first three rungs of this Biblical symbol as representing faith, hope and charity.

LAMB

This symbol of ingenuous innocence and of sacrifice has a lineage from the Lamb of God and was adopted as an icon of the Knights Templar.

LEVEL

An early precursor of a spirit level to ensure horizontal surfaces are level, this operative tool stands for equality.

MAUL

This thick wooden mallet represents brute force and so was the murder weapon that the Temple conspirators used to slay Hiram Abiff.

Masonic apron

The initial clean white apron is emblematic of innocence and purity of the soul. English Masonic aprons have a blue border symbolizing the Blue Lodge and blue rosettes are added as the Fellow Craft and Master Mason degrees are passed.

Mosaic Pavement

The chess board black-and-white floor of a lodge symbolizing the rewards and pitfalls of earthly existence.

Northeast

The northeast corner of a lodge symbolizes new growth as stonemasons always laid the first cornerstone of a new building in this corner.

Pillars

The two pillars, Jachin and Boaz, found in every Masonic lodge in honour of King Solomon's Temple. They are topped with globes representing the earth – or, sometimes, heaven.

Plumb

The plumb line was a weight on a line of string used by operative Masons to ascertain that a wall was straight and thus represents upright, conscientious behaviour.

Pot of Incense

An emblem for a pure heart and giving appreciation to the Great Architect of the Universe.

Scythe

This portentous tool has the same significance in Masonic symbolism as when it is carried by the Grim Reaper – an imminent demise.

Slipper

Candidates for the Entered Apprentice and Fellow Craft degree enter the lodge wearing one slipper. They have emblematically given the other one to the Craft as a sign of their good intentions and sincerity.

Square

The most intrinsic of all Masonic symbols, evoking honesty, truth and virtue.

Supports of the Lodge

Freemasons' lodges are said to be supported by the three pillars of Wisdom, Strength and Beauty. These correspond to the senior lodge officers – the Worshipful Master, Senior Warden and Junior Warden.

Trowel

This humble tool, used to spread cement between bricks, represents the bond of love and knowledge that unites Masons.

Tyler's Sword and the Book of Constitutions

The Tyler's sword – never sheathed – stands for eternal vigilance against hostile forces. When laid across the movement's *magnum opus*, it signifies taking equal care of the fraternity's spiritual core.

Volume of Sacred Law

The King James Bible or another Holy Book is opened while the lodge is in session to remind members to live by its strictures at all times.

WINDING STAIRCASE

Part of the Fellow Craft degree symbolizing passing to the Middle Chamber of King Solomon's Temple. The first three stairs represent the three Blue Lodge degrees; the second five steps stand for the five schools of classical architecture; and the final seven stairs evoke the seven liberal arts.

FAMOUS
FREEMASONS

WILLIAM 'BUD' ABBOTT (1897–1974) American
  actor and comedian and one-half of the Abbott
  & Costello comedy duo.

HAROLD ABRAHAMS (1899–1978) British athlete
  who won the 100 metre gold medal at the 1924
  Olympics. This was later dramatized in the 1981
  movie *Chariots of Fire*.

BUZZ ALDRIN (1930–) American astronaut who
  was the second man to walk on the moon.

SALVADOR ALLENDE (1908–73) President of
  Chile who was ousted from power by General
  Pinochet.

ROALD AMUNDSEN (1872–1928) Norwegian
  explorer who in 1911 led the first successful
  expedition to the South Pole.

LOUIS ARMSTRONG (1901–71) American jazz
  trumpeter and singer known as 'Satchmo'.

THOMAS ARNE (1710–78) English composer of
'Rule Britannia'.

ELIAS ASHMOLE (1617–92) Founder of the Royal
Society and the Ashmolean Museum in Oxford.

MUSTAFA ATATURK (1881–1938) Founder and
first President of Turkey.

STEPHEN AUSTIN (1793–1836) Lawyer and
colonist known as the 'Father of Texas'.

GENE AUTRY (1907–98) American performer and
singer known as the 'Singing Cowboy'.

DR THOMAS BARNADO (1845–1905)
Philanthropist and founder of Barnado's
childrens' homes.

'COUNT' WILLIAM BASIE (1904–84) US jazz
pianist, organist and leader of the Count Basie
Orchestra.

EDMUND BARTON (1849–1920) Politician, judge
and first Prime Minister of Australia.

IRVING BERLIN (1888–1989) Siberian-born, US-
based composer of 'White Christmas' and
Annie, Get Your Gun.

MEL BLANC (1908–89) US radio actor and voice of
animated characters such as Bugs Bunny, Daffy
Duck and Sylvester.

SIMON BOLIVAR (1783-1830) South American revolutionary and first post-colonial President of Bolivia. Founded a lodge in Peru.

ERNEST BORGNINE (1917-) American film and TV actor and Academy Award winner.

JAMES BOWIE (1796-1836) American pioneer who died at the Alamo and gave his name to the Bowie knife.

JAMES BUCHANAN (1791-1868) Fifteenth President of the United States.

EDMUND BURKE (1729-97) Anglo-Irish statesman and supporter of the pre-Revolution American colonies.

ROBERT BURNS (1759-96) Scottish poet, bard and composer of copious Masonic poems and songs.

SIR WILLIAM 'BILLY' BUTLIN (1899-1980) British founder of Butlins holiday camps.

LORD BYRON (1788-1824) Romantic poet, libertine and Grand Master of the Premier Grand Lodge of Freemasons (1747-52).

DONALD CAMPBELL (1921-67) English car and motorboat racer who crashed and died while trying to set a new world water speed record. Son of Malcolm.

SIR MALCOLM CAMPBELL (1885–1948) English
holder of land and water speed records during
the 1920s and 1930s.

GEORGE CANNING (1770–1827) Former British
Prime Minister.

GIACOMO CASANOVA (1725–98) Italian rake and
socialite.

WALTER CHRYSLER (1875–1940) American
founder of the Chrysler Corporation automobile
company. He also built New York's Chrysler
Building.

SIR WINSTON CHURCHILL (1874–1965) British
Prime Minister during the Second World War.

ANDRE CITROËN (1878–1935) French founder of
the Citroën car company.

WILLIAM CODY (1846–1917) aka 'Buffalo Bill',
founder of the touring American 'Wild West
Show'.

NAT 'KING' COLE (1919–65) American singer and
jazz musician.

CARLO COLLODI (1826–90) Italian writer who
created Pinocchio.

SAMUEL COLT (1814–62) Inventor of the Colt
revolver.

LESLIE COMPTON (1912–84) Arsenal and England

footballer who also played cricket for
Middlesex.

SIR ARTHUR CONAN DOYLE (1859–1930)
Author of the Sherlock Holmes detective
stories.

DAVY CROCKETT (1786–1836) Texan politician
and rebel who died at the Alamo.

JIM DAVIDSON (1953–) English comedian who
resigned as Worshipful Master of Chelsea
Lodge, London in 2002 after complaints about
blue material when he performed at a gala
dinner.

ROGER DE COURCEY (1944–) English
ventriloquist famous for his sidekick Nookie
the Bear.

CECIL B DE MILLE (1881–1959) Early twentieth
century American film director.

JACK DEMPSEY (1895–1983) US boxer and
heavyweight world champion from 1919–26.

BOB DOLE (1923–) American Republican senator
defeated in the 1996 Presidential election by Bill
Clinton.

JEAN HENRI DUNANT (1828–1910) Swiss founder
of the Red Cross.

PETER EBDON (1970–) English snooker player.

EDWARD VII (1841–1910) King of Great Britain and Ireland from 1901–10. Became a Masonic Grand Master in 1874.

EDWARD VIII (1894–1972) King of Great Britain and Ireland from January 1936 until abdication in December 1936.

ALEXANDRE GUSTAVE EIFFEL (1832–1923) French architect who designed the Eiffel Tower.

EDWARD KENNEDY 'DUKE' ELLINGTON (1899–1974) US jazz pianist and bandleader.

DOUGLAS FAIRBANKS SNR (1883–1939) American star of silent movies such as *The Mark of Zorro* and *The Thief of Baghdad.*

W C FIELDS (1880–1946) American comedian and comic-actor.

GEOFFREY FISHER (1887–1972) Archbishop of Canterbury from 1945–61.

SIR ALEXANDER FLEMING (1881–1955) Scottish biologist who won the Nobel Prize for discovering penicillin.

CYRIL FLETCHER (1913–2005) English comedian, entertainer and composer of 'Odd Odes'.

GERALD FORD (1913–) Thirty-eighth President of the United States.

HENRY FORD (1863–1947) Founder of the Ford Motor Company.

BENJAMIN FRANKLIN (1706–90) American politician, diplomat and Founding Father.

CLARK GABLE (1901–60) US actor and star of *Gone With The Wind* and *Mutiny On The Bounty*.

DAVID GARRICK (1717–79) English actor, dramatist and theatrical producer.

GIUSEPPE GARIBALDI (1807–82) Italian military leader and statesman.

RICHARD J GATLING (1818–1903) Inventor of the Gatling gun.

GEORGE IV (1762–1830) King of Great Britain and Ireland from 1820–30. Grand Master of Grand Lodge of England from 1790–1813.

GEORGE VI (1895–1952) King of Great Britain and Ireland from 1935–52. Honorary Past Grand Master of United Grand Lodge of England.

EDWARD GIBBON (1734–94) English historian and author of *The History of the Decline and Fall of the Roman Empire*.

SIR WILLIAM GILBERT (1836–1911) English co-composer of light operas with fellow-Freemason Sir Arthur Sullivan.

JOHN GLENN (1921–) American astronaut and
Democrat Senator.

BARRY GOLDWATER (1909–98) US Republican
Senator for Arizona and 1964 Presidential
candidate.

JOHANN WOLFGANG VON GOETHE
(1749–1832) German dramatist, poet and
philosopher.

DR JOSEPH-IGNACE GUILLOTIN (1738–1814)
French physician, politician and inventor of the
guillotine.

FIELD MARSHAL SIR DOUGLAS HAIG
(1861–1928) British military commander during
the First World War.

ALEX HALEY (1921–92) American author of *The
Autobiography of Malcolm X* and *Roots.*

WARREN G HARDING (1865–1923) Twenty-ninth
President of the United States.

OLIVER HARDY (1892–1957) American actor and
comedian and one half of Laurel & Hardy comic
duo.

JOSEF HAYDN (1732–1809) Austrian composer
introduced to Freemasonry by Mozart.

JOSIAH HENSON (1789–1883) Black American
who escaped from slavery and was the

inspiration for Harriet Beecher Stowe's novel *Uncle Tom's Cabin.*

JAMES HOBAN (1762–1831) Irish architect who designed the original White House and its replacement.

WILLIAM HOGARTH (1697–1764) British painter, cartoonist and satirist.

J EDGAR HOOVER (1895–1972) Founder of America's Federal Bureau of Investigations (FBI).

BOB HOPE (1903–2003) British-American comedian and entertainer.

HARRY HOUDINI (1874–1926) Legendary escapologist.

KING HUSSEIN OF JORDAN (1935–99) King of Jordan from 1952–99.

SIR LEONARD HUTTON (1916–90) Yorkshire and England cricket captain.

BURL IVES (1909–95) American folk singer, writer and actor.

ANDREW JACKSON (1767–1845) Seventh President of the United States and founder of the Democratic Party.

REV. JESSE JACKSON (1941–) American minister, politician and civil rights activist.

ANDREW JOHNSON (1808–75) Seventeenth
President of the United States.

JACK JOHNSON (1878–1946) First black
heavyweight boxing champion of the world,
from 1908–15.

LYNDON B JOHNSON (1908–73) Thirty-sixth
President of the United States.

AL JOLSON (1886–1950) American singer and
entertainer.

BENITO JUAREZ (1806–72) President of Mexico
from 1861–63 and 1867–72.

KING DAVID KALAKAUA (1836–91) The last king
of the Hawaiian kingdom.

EDMUND KEAN (1787–1833) English
Shakespearean actor.

RUDYARD KIPLING (1865–1936) British poet and
author famous for *The Jungle Book*.

LORD HORATIO HERBERT KITCHENER (1850–
1916) British military leader and politician.

MARQUIS DE LAFAYETTE (1757–1834) French
aristocrat heavily involved in both French and
American revolutions.

FIORELLO LAGUARDIA (1882–1947) Renowned
mayor of New York who left his name to one of
the city's airports.

SIR HARRY LAUDER (1870–1950) Scottish entertainer and music hall artist.

CHARLES LINDBERGH (1902–74) American aviator who made the first non-stop flight from the US to Europe.

SIR THOMAS LIPTON (1850–1931) Scottish yachtsman who also created the Lipton Tea Company.

FRANZ LIZST (1811–86) Hungarian composer and pianist.

SIR CLIVE LLOYD (1944–) Former West Indies cricket captain.

HAROLD LLOYD (1893–1971) American actor famous for his comic silent movies.

DOUGLAS MACARTHUR (1880–1964) American general and military leader.

JAMES MADISON (1751–1836) Fourth President of the United States.

ALFRED MARKS (1921–96) English actor.

GEORGE C MARSHALL (1880–1959) American general who formulated the Marshall Plan for Europe's post-Second World War reconstruction.

HARPO MARX (1888–1964) Harp-playing, non-speaking Marx Brother.

WILLIAM MCKINLEY (1843–1901) Twenty-fifth President of the United States.

JACKIE MILBURN (1924–88) Newcastle United and England footballer.

JAMES MONROE (1758–1831) Fifth President of the United States.

WOLFGANG AMADEUS MOZART (1756–91) Austrian composer who wrote a Masonic opera, *The Magic Flute*, and the litany *Masonic Funeral Music*.

AUDIE MURPHY (1924–71) America's most decorated Second World War hero who later became an actor.

DAVID NIXON (1919–78) English magician and television entertainer.

ARNOLD PALMER (1929–) American golfer.

JAMES C PENNEY (1875–1971) Founder of the J C Penney chain of US retail stores.

ALBERT PIKE (1809–91) US Confederate military officer and Masonic philosopher who formalized the Scottish Rite.

JAMES KNOX POLK (1795–1849) Eleventh President of the United States.

ALEXANDER POPE (1688–1744) English poet and satirist.

RICHARD PRYOR (1940–2005) American comedian and actor.

ALEKSANDR PUSHKIN (1799–1837) Russian author and poet.

RONALD REAGAN (1911–2004) Fortieth President of the United States. Although he was never a Blue Lodge Mason, Reagan was made an 'Honorary Scottish Rite Mason' in 1988.

MICHAEL RICHARDS (1949–) US actor who played Cosmo Kramer in *Seinfeld*.

'SUGAR' RAY ROBINSON (1921–89) American boxer and world middleweight and welterweight champion.

ROY ROGERS (1911–98) American singer and star of cowboy movies.

FRANKLIN D ROOSEVELT (1882–1945) Thirty-second President of the United States and inventor of the 'New Deal'.

THEODORE ROOSEVELT (1858–1919) Twenty-sixth President of the United States.

NATHAN MAYER ROTHSCHILD (1777–1836) German-born founder of the Rothschild banking dynasty.

'COLONEL' HARLAND SANDERS (1890–1980)

Founder of the Kentucky Fried Chicken fast food chain.

TELLY SAVALAS (1924–94) Greek-American actor best known for playing TV detective *Kojak*.

ROBERT FALCON SCOTT (1868–1912) British explorer known as Scott of the Antarctic.

SIR WALTER SCOTT (1771–1832) Scottish novelist and poet and author of *Ivanhoe*.

PETER SELLERS (1925–80) British actor and comedian.

SIR ERNEST SHACKLETON (1874–1922) British explorer.

LEN SHACKLETON (1922–2000) Sunderland and England footballer.

REV. AL SHARPTON (1954–) American politician and civil rights activist.

JEAN SIBELIUS (1865–1957) Finnish composer.

SIR ARTHUR SULLIVAN (1842–1900) British composer of light operas with fellow Freemason Sir William Gilbert.

JOCK STEIN (1922–85) Glasgow Celtic and Scotland football manager.

HERBERT SUTCLIFFE (1894–1978) Yorkshire and England cricketer.

JONATHAN SWIFT (1667-1745) Irish writer and satirist and author of *Gulliver's Travels*.

WILLIAM H. TAFT (1857-1930) Twenty-seventh President of the United States.

TOMMY TRINDER (1909-89) English comedian and actor.

ANTHONY TROLLOPE (1815-82) English novelist and inventor of the red postbox.

HARRY S. TRUMAN (1884-1972) Thirty-third President of the United States.

MARK TWAIN (1835-1910) American satirist, writer and author of *The Adventures of Tom Sawyer*.

VOLTAIRE (real name: FRANCOIS-MARIE AROUET) (1694-1778) French writer, satirist and philosopher.

ROBERT PERSHING WADLOW (1918-40) American who was the tallest man of modern times, standing eight foot eleven inches.

GEORGE C WALLACE (1919-98) US Democrat segregationist Governor of Alabama.

JACK L WARNER (1892-1978) Founder and president of Warner Brother Studios.

GEORGE WASHINGTON (1732-99) First President of the United States.

JOHN WAYNE (1907–79) American actor, star of Western movies.

CAPTAIN MATTHEW WEBB (1848–83) Englishman who in 1875 became the first man to swim the English Channel.

ARTHUR WELLESLEY, DUKE OF WELLINGTON (1759–1862) British military leader and statesman.

OSCAR WILDE (1854–1900) Irish playwright and novelist.

WILLIAM IV (1765–1837) King of Great Britain and Ireland from 1830–37.

STEVE WOZNIAK (1950–) Co-founder with Steve Jobs of Apple Computer.

SIR CHRISTOPHER WREN (1632–1723) English architect who designed many of London's churches, including St Paul's Cathedral.

DARRYL F ZANUCK (1902–79) US founder of Twentieth Century Fox.

INDEX

A-Z of famous Freemasons
232–47
Aaron 19
Abiff, Hiram 18, 20, 21–5,
54, 73, 78, 93, 120, 141,
154, 161, 186–90, 193
Abraham 17
Adam and Eve 48, 184
African Lodge (US) 63
Age of Enlightenment 37
al-Aqsa Intifada 17
al-Aqsa Mosque 25, 84, 88
Alabama 119
Alexandria Lodge
(Washington DC) 106
America see United States
American Civil War
(1861–65) 68, 69
American War of
Independence (1775–83)
63–4, 103, 118
Amiens 31

Ancient Arabic Nobles of
the Mystic Shrine 70
Ancient Charges see
Constitution, History etc
Anderson, Dr James 47–50,
77, 102, 104
Andrae, Johann Valentin
100–01
Anglo Masonry 56, 60
The Anti-Christ and the
Origin of Masonry 115
anti-Masonic Party (US)
67–8
Antient Grand Lodge 47
Antients vs Moderns 47,
53–4, 56–7, 207
Apple Tree tavern (Covent
Garden) 44
apron 140–42
Fellow Craft 174
Master Mason 185
Ark of the Covenant 19, 24

Ashmole, Elias 42, 99, 233
Athelstan, King 33-5, 73
Australia 5

Babylonians 24-5
Bacon, Sir Francis 99
Baigent, Michael 90
Bannockburn, Battle of
    (1314) 91
Baphomet 114, 115
Bathsheba 17
Bavaria 111, 113
Beeston, Mark 112, 219-20
Beethoven, Ludwig van 100
Benedict XVI, Pope 53
Bernhard, Prince 123
biblical origins 7, 12, 15-16,
    77
Bildberg Group 123
Black, Conrad 123
black-balling 145
Blair, Tony 123
Blue Lodge 134, 141, 143,
    146, 199
Book of Constitution *see*
    *The Constitution, History,
    Laws, Charges, orders,
    regulations and Usages of*

*the Right Worshipful
    Fraternity of Accepted
    Free Masons, collected
    from their General records
    and their Faithful
    Traditions of Many Ages*
Boston Tea Party (1773) 64,
    73, 102, 103
British Museum 32
*The Brotherhood and the
    Manipulation of Society*
    (Fraser & Beeston)
    219-20
Brown, Dan 1-3, 4, 8, 24,
    25, 42-3, 57, 73-4, 75,
    76, 83, 87-8, 94-5, 96,
    102, 103-06, 107, 108-09,
    110, 113, 122, 205
Bunker Hill 103
Bush, George H.W. 66, 123
Bush, George W. 123

cable-tow 151
Canada 5
Canterbury Cathedral 31
Capitol building
    (Washington DC) 65
Carter, Jimmy 66

Chapter of the Rose Croix
214–15
Knight of the East 214
Knight of the East and
West 214
Knight of the Rose Croix
214
Prince of Jerusalem 214
The Charges of a Free
Mason 48–9
democracy 50
forbidding of discussion
on religion and politics
50–1
influence of 48
internal harmony 50
non-specific deism of 49
patriotism 50
peaceable subjects 50
as summation of existing
Masonic law 50
Chartres 31
Chile 117
Chivalric Masonry 208–09
Illustrious Order of the
Red Cross 209
Order of Malta 209
Order of the Temple 210

Churchill, Sir Winston 71,
73, 235
Clement V, Pope 85, 86, 89
Clement VI, Pope 115
Clement XII, Pope 52
Clinton, Bill 123
Clinton, Dewitt 67
Code of Canon Law (1917) 53
collegia see Roman Colleges
of Architects
colonial Lodges 62
Columbus, Christopher 97
Comacine Masons
(Comacine Masters) 80–2
Como, Lake 80
Comyn, John 90
Consistory Degrees 217–18
*Constitution, History, Laws,
Charges, Orders,
Regulations and Usages of
the Right Worshipful
Fraternity of Accepted
Free Masons, collected
from their General records
and their Faithful
Traditions of Many Ages*
48–51, 52, 77, 102, 104
Cooke Manuscript 38

Cooke, Matthew 38
Copper Scroll 89
Council of Kadosh 215–17
  Chief of the Tabernacle
    217
  Grand Pontiff 216
  Knight of the Brazen
    Street 217
  Knight Commander of the
    Temple 217
  Knight of Kadosh 217
  Knight of the Royal Axe,
    Prince of Libanus 216–17
  Knight of the Sun 217
  Master of Symbolic Lodge
    216
  Noachite 216
  Prince of Mercy 217
  Prince of the tabernacle
    217
  Scottish Knight of St
    Andrew 217
Council of Royal and Select
  Masters 207
cowans 136
the Craft see Freemasonry
cronyism 121–22
Crowley, Aleister 87

Crown tavern (Drury Lane)
    44
Crusades (1096–1250) 83–4
Cryptic Rite 207–08
  Royal Master 208
  Select Master 208
  Super Excellent Master
    208
Czechoslovakia 71

The Da Vinci Code (Brown)
    1–2, 25, 87–8, 94, 115,
    205
David, King 17
Dead Sea Scrolls 89
Deacons 143
Declaration of
    Independence (1776) 64,
    104–05
degree ceremonies 143–46
  appendant 198–99
  Entered Apprentice
    147–63
  Fellow Craft 164–77
  Master Mason 177–97
Degrees of Areopagus 215
Dermott, Laurence 47
devil worship 114–16

Dionysian Artificers *see* Fraternity of Dionysian Artificers

Dome on the Rock 25

dress code 139–40

Edward II 91

Edward III 30

Edwin 34

Eisenhower, Dwight D. 66

Elks 4

Ely Cathedral 31

encyclical Humanum Genus (1884) 52

Entered Apprentice 10, 21, 35, 49, 54, 93, 134, 140, 146

Entered Apprentice Degree Ceremony 147–62
 Apron Lecture 159–60
 circumambulation 152
 Due-Guard 154–55
 Grip 156–58
 Lecture 161–62
 Obligation 152–53
 Sign 155–56

Essenes 89, 97

Ethiopia 189

Euclid 33

Fellow Craft 10, 21, 35, 54, 134, 146

Fellow Craft Degree Ceremony 164–77
 Due-Guard 167–68
 Obligation 167
 Pass-Grip 170–71
 Real Grip 171–74
 Sign 169

Festive Board 131, 163

fifteen articles (Regius Manuscript)
 acceptance of commission 36
 attendance of chapter 35
 love of God 36
 oath of commitment to the Craft 36
 patriotism 36
 payment of workers 35
 peace-making 36
 prohibition on stealing 36
 recruitment procedures 35–6

relationship with Fellows of the Craft/Entered Apprentices 35

serene and contemplative behaviour 36

sleeping with fellow Mason's wife 36

truth, honesty and reliability 35, 37

withholding of trade secrets 36

Five Points of Fellowship 195–96

Florence 31

four cardinal virtues 162

France 31, 51, 55, 71, 95

Antients vs Moderns squabble 56–7

and devotion to non-denominational Supreme being 59

expansion in 58

Jacobite connection 56

Knights Templar theory 57

Masonry forced underground 58

popularity/size of lodges 60

women and non-believers admitted 59–60

Franco, Francisco 117

Franklin, Benjamin 64, 104, 105, 111

Fraser, Ivan 112, 219–20

Fraternity of Dionysian Artificers 18, 78–80, 87, 88, 100, 122

Frederick Lewis, Prince of Wales 51

Fredericksburg (Virginia) 106

Free Stone Masons 29

Freemasonry

appeal of 2–3

beliefs 8–9, 12

as benevolent philosophical movement 5–6

ceremonies 6

Christian/Medieval roots 7, 12, 15–16

corruption in 13, 122

decline 3, 5

description of 4–5

differing views on 3–4

fear/suspicion of 15

Freemasonry – *cont.*
  fifteen articles 32–7
  financial fortunes 39
  guild system 29–32
  joining 9–10, 14
  levels of 11–12
  male-only bastion 11
  motivations 6
  origins of term 29
  path to enlightenment 10
  post-war image 72–3
  progressive thinkers 40–4
  regular meetings of 7–8
  ridicule of 6–7
  secretiveness of 13–14
  social status 39
Freemasonry Watch 119
French Revolution 73, 105

Gates, Bill 123
Geometry 128
George II 32, 51
George III 104
Gettysburg, Battle of (1863) 69
Goose & Gridiron tavern (London) 44, 45–6
Gothic style 26–9, 31, 38, 81

Grand Architect of the Universe 7
Grand Elect Perfect and Sublime degree 213
Grand Lodge of All England (York) 46, 199
Grand Lodge of England (London) 46, 51, 54, 62
Grand Lodge of Ireland 46
Grand Lodge of Masons (York) 34, 199
Grand Lodge of Massachusetts 63
Grand Lodge of St John of Scotland 46
Grand Lodge of Scotland 62
Grand Lodges 8, 14, 112
  founding of 44–6
  France 56, 58–60
  recognition of 61
  US 69
  see also Masonic Lodges
Grand Master 85, 92, 137
  first appointment 45–6
  King Solomon as Most Excellent Master 78
Grand Orient de France 56, 58–60

Grand Procession 191
Grande Loge Nationale
    Francaise 60
grave 193
Great Fire of London (1666)
    43
Great (Grand) Architect of
    the Universe 49, 59, 128
Great Seal 76
Great Seal of America
    108–11, 112
Green Dragon tavern
    (Boston) 62, 64, 102–03
guilds 73
  and inculcation of
    moral/personal
    behaviour 32
  legislation against 30–1
  move to
    philosophical/moral
    fraternity 40–4
  role 29–30
  setting up of 29–32
Guillotine, Dr Joseph 59
Gull, Dr William 120

Hall, Manly 79
Hall, Prince 63

Halliwell, James 33
Halliwell Manuscript *see*
    Regius Manuscript
Hamill, John 95–6
Hancock, John 103, 104
Hanks, Tom 1, 94
Henry VIII 38
Hewes, Joseph 104
Hiram I, King of Tyre 18,
    19, 20, 24, 161
Hiramic legend 20–5
Hitler, Adolf 71, 116, 117
*The Holy Blood and the Holy
    Grail* (Baigent, Leigh,
    Lincoln) 90
Holy Grail 25, 76, 87, 88,
    205
Holy Lands 83–4, 100
Holy Royal Arch 54
Hooper, William 104
Hugues de Payens (aka Yves
    de Faillon) 84
Hussein, Saddam 117
Hutton, Will 123

Icke, David 122
Illuminati 110, 111–12,
    113

Immediate Past Master 138–40

India 5, 51

Inquisition 15, 52

Inspector General 319

Iraq 117

Ireland 5

Islam *see* Muslims

Israel 5

Italy 31, 52, 71, 117

Jachin 174

Jack the Ripper 120–21

Jack the Ripper: The Final Solution (Knight) 120

Jacobites 56

Jahbulon 204, 206

James II 56

James VI of Scotland 40, 41

Japan 5

Jefferson, Thomas 104, 107

Jerusalem 16, 83–4, 95, 105

Jesus 17

jewels 141–42, 161

Jewish conspiracy theory 116–17

John the Evangelist 109

Jubela 21–3, 120, 154, 155, 188, 189

Jubelo 21–3, 120, 189

Jubelum 21–3, 120, 189

Junior Deacon 132, 146

Junior Grand Deacon 139

Junior Grand Steward 139

Junior Warden 125, 127, 130–31

Kabbalah 206, 216

Kadosh 215–17

Kilwinning Lodge No 40

King Solomon's Temple *see* Temple of Solomon

Knight, Christopher 93–4, 96

Knight, Stephen 120

Knights of Malta 220

Knights Templar 3, 57, 62, 68, 76, 114, 220

allegations against 85–6

aprons worn by 140

arrival in Scotland 90-2

connection with Masons 89–92

connections with America 96–8, 108

evicted from Middle East
85
novelistic interpretations
90
origins 83–4
pardoned by Pope Clement
V 86
and Rosslyn 95
and Sangreal documents
87–8
secrets of 86–8
wealth of 84–5
Koran 17
Ku Klux Klan 118–19

Lafayette, Marquis de 105,
107
Lake Ontario 67
Latin America 5
Leadbeater, C.W. 87
Leigh, Richard 90
L'Enfant, Pierre Charles 107
Leo XII, Pope 52, 115
Leonardo Da Vinci 100
Lion of Judah 195
lions 136
Livingston, Robert 64
Lodge of Perfection 212–14

Loge de Neuf Soeurs (Lodge
of Nine Sisters) (Paris)
105
loggia 80
Lomas, Robert 93–4, 96–8
Lost Word 204
Low Countries 31
Lucifer 114
Luther, Martin 38

McCarthy, Senator 68
Magistri Comacini see
Comacine Masons
(Comacine Masters)
Mahmah 184
Major, John 123
Mandaeans 97
Masonic anthem 163
The Masonic Assassins 115
Masonic Constitution 47–51
Masonic Lodges 39–40
countrywide scattering of
43
derivation 125
entry into 40–3
expansion of 51
foreign 51
layout 124–28

Masonic Lodges – *cont.*
  in London 43
  meetings held at 129
  responsibilities and duties
    of members 41
  ritual/symbolic
    observance in 43–4
  symbolism in 124–26
  in US 119
  see also Grand Lodges
Masons' Livery Company 28
masons, medieval
  considered miracle
    workers 27, 28, 37–9
  and crisis in the Church
    38–9
  effect of Renaissance/Age
    of Enlightenment on
    37–9
  and explosion of church
    building 26
  and Gothic style 26–8
  lack of work 39
  Livery Company 28
  and printing presses 37
  skills of 28
  trade guilds 29–32
Massachusetts 62

Master Mason Degree
    Ceremony 177–97
  Due-Guard 181
  Obligation 180–81
  Pass-Grip 181–85
  Sign 181
Master Masons 6, 10, 21, 54,
    65, 134, 141, 146
  control of 28
  fifteen articles 35–7
  influence/importance of
    31
  and setting up of guilds
    29–30
  signs and grips 30
  training of 29–30
maul/gavel 188
Mercury 132
Middle East 78, 85, 117
Milan 31
Modern School 54
Mohammed 17
Molay, Jacques de 85–6
Moray, Robert 99
Morgan, William 67–8
Moses 19, 48, 75
Most Excellent Grand
    Master 78

Most Worshipful Grand
   Master 139
Mount Moriah 16–17, 24–5,
   25, 78, 84, 87, 92, 97
Muslims 17, 25, 70, 83, 84,
   85, 105
Mussolini, Benito 71, 117

Napoleon Bonaparte 58
Nebuchadnezzar, King 24
The New Atlantis (Bacon)
   99–100
New Mexico 65
New World Order 8, 76,
   111–14, 117
The New World Order
   (Robertson) 113
Newton, Sir Isaac 100
Noah 48
Noah's Ark 37, 81, 82
Northern Masonic
   Jurisdiction (NMI) (US)
   212
Notre-Dame (Paris) 31, 86
Nova Scotia 98

Oklahoma 119
operative Masons 41, 43–4

The Ordeal 145
Order of Malta 209
Order of the Temple 210
Osiris 193
Oxbrow, Mark 95

Palestine 85
Palladism 114
Paris 56, 114
Payne, Robert 104
Philip IV 89, 115
Philippines 5
Phoenicians 19
Pike, Albert 57, 68, 114,
   118
Pinochet, Augusto 117
Poland 71
Pompeii 80
Poor Knights of Christ 84
Porritt, Jonathan 123
Portugal 52
Prince Hall Masons 63, 118,
   119
printing press 37
Private Eye 122
Protestant reformation
   38
Protestantism 52

The Protocols of the Elders
   of Zion 116
Pythagoras 79, 82, 89, 143

Ramsay, Andrew Michael 57
Ramsay Oration 57
Red Cross (Croix) 215
Reformation of
   Freemasonry 54–5
Regius Manuscript (1390)
   48, 77, 199
 Christian fables 37
 connection with Athelstan
   33–5
 emphasis on
   spiritual/self-
   improvement aspects 36,
   37
 and fable of four Masons
   36–7
 fifteen articles of 35–6
 given to British Museum
   32
 as poem on professional,
   moral, philosophical
   behaviour 32
 and science of geometry
   33

Renaissance 37, 43, 110
Revere, Paul 103
ritual 6, 38, 54–5, 65, 68
Robert the Bruce 90, 91
Robertson, Ian 95
Robertson, Pat 113
Rockefeller, David 123
Rod of Aaron 19
Roman Catholic Church
   26–7, 38–9, 52–5, 84–5
Roman Colleges of
   Architects 79–80
Rome 90, 114
Roosevelt, Franklin D. 72
Rosenkreuz, Christian 100,
   101, 215
Rosicrucians 100–02
Rosslyn Chapel 92–6, 98
Rosslyn and the Grail
   (Oxbrow & Robertson) 95
Rotary Club 4
Rouen 31
Rough Masons 29
Royal Arch Masonry 200
 Mark Master 200–01
 Most Excellent Master 201
 Past Master 201
 Royal Arch 201–06

Royal Freemasons 51
Royal Society of London 42
Rummer & Grapes tavern (Westminster) 44
Rumsfeld, Donald 123

St Andrew's Lodge No 82 (Boston) 62, 102
St John's Grand Lodge (Boston) 62
St John's Lodge Bible 66
St John's Lodge No 1 (New York) 66
St Paul's Cathedral 44, 45
Sangreal documents 87-8, 94, 97
Sayer, Anthony 46
Schaw Statutes 41
Schaw, William 41
Scotland 5, 40, 46, 90-1, 98
Scottish Rite 11, 12, 55, 65, 68, 94, 109, 110, 114, 210-12
Sea-Faring Man 189
Seal of Solomon 109
seating plan
    Almoner 137
    Chaplain 136
    Charity Steward 137-38
    Director of Ceremonies 137
    Inner Guard 133
    Junior Deacon 132
    Junior Steward 133-34
    Junior Warden 130-31
    Organist 138
    Secretary 135
    Senior Deacon 132
    Senior Steward 133
    Senior Warden 130
    Treasurer 135
    Tyler 135
    Worshipful Master 129-30
The Second Messiah: Templars, the Turin Shroud and the Great Secret of Freemasonry (Knight & Lomas) 93-4, 96-8
Second World War 71
Senior Deacon 132, 145
Senior Warden 125, 126, 127, 130
Sharon, Ariel 16
shibboleth 173
Shriners 70

Siena 31

Sinclair, Sir William 92

slipshod 180

Solomon Key 205–06

The Solomon Key (Brown) 2, 4, 24, 73–4, 94–5, 96, 103–06, 107, 108–09

Solomon, King 17–19, 20, 22–3, 24, 78, 81, 109, 161, 189, 194

Sons of Solomon 79

South America 51

Southeast Asia 51

Southern Masonic Jurisdiction (SMI) (US) 211–12

Soviet Union 117

Spain 31, 51, 52, 71, 117

speculative Masons 41–3, 93

Spielberg, Stephen 123

Spiritus Sanctum 101

Stirling Castle 91

Stockton, Richard 104

stonemasons 12, 15

Symbolic Lodge 134

symbols 8, 38

  3 222

  24-inch gauge 221

47th Proposition of Euclid 222

acacia 222

all-seeing eye 222–23

anchor and the Ark 223

ashlars 223

beehive 223

cable-tow 223

chalk, charcoal and clay 224

circumambulation 152, 224

coffin and spade 224

compass 127, 224

corn, wine and oil 224–25

cornucopia 225

double-headed eagle 225

five-pointed blazing star 162, 225

G 225

gavel 188, 226

heart and sword 226

hoodwink 226

hourglass 226

indented tassel 161–62, 226–27

Jacob's ladder 227

lamb 227

level 227
Masonic apron 228
maul 188, 227
mosaic pavement 161, 228
northeast 228
pillars 228
plumb 229
pot of incense 229
scythe 229
slipper 229
square 229
square and compass 127, 128
supports of the Lodge 230
trowel 230
Tyler's Sword and Book of Constitutions 230
Volume of Sacred Law 230
winding staircase 231
Syria 85

33rd Degree 219-20
Tatou, Audrey 1, 94
Taxil, Leo 114-16
Taylor, Greg 110
The Temple and the Lodge (Baigent & Leigh) 90

Temple of Solomon 38, 75, 78-9, 83, 84, 87, 88, 89, 117, 180
aprons worn at 140
building of 16-20
destruction of 24-5
Jachin and Boaz pillars 19, 92, 126
layout of 19
Lodges based upon 125
Pillar of Beauty 213
rebuilding of 25
remains of 25
Rosslyn as replica of 94
treasure from 95
Tetragrammaton 213
Thatcher, Margaret 123
Third degree 178
Three Great Lights 127, 147-48
Three Precious Jewels 176
Attentive Ear 176
Faithful Breast 176
Instructive Tongue 176
Tower of Babel 37
Tracing Board 127, 128
Truman, Harry S. 72

Tubulcain 184
Tyler 135, 136, 140, 143

United Grand Lodge of
    England (UGLE) 47,
    54-5, 95-6, 127
United States 51, 55
    47th Proposition of Euclid
    143
    African Lodge in 63
    competing Grand Lodges
    in 62
    detractors of Masons in
    66
    founding a nation 103-06
    growth in 65
    Independence Day 104-05
    Masonic Emblem on Great
    Seal 108-11
    as Masonic project 96-106
    Morgan scandal 67-8
    New World Order 111-14
    ostracism of Masons 68
    Past Masters 139
    post-Civil War
    rehabilitation 68-70
    pre-Columbus Templars
    96-106

role of Masons in history
    of 61-5
Scottish Rite in 211-12
square-and-compass
    image 128
War of Independence 62,
    64
Washington DC as
    Masonic road map
    107-08
York Rite in 200
Uriah 17

Vatican 53, 86
Victoria, Queen 120
Voltaire, F.M. Arouet de
    105
Volume of Sacred Law 126,
    127, 132, 136, 148

Wailing Wall 25
Wales 5
Wallace, George 119
Walton, George 104
Warren, Joseph 103
Washington DC 106-08
Washington, George 4, 65,
    66, 73, 106, 107

Weishaupt, Adam 112, 113
Wells Cathedral 31
Westminster Abbey 31
Whipple, William 104
Winchester Cathedral 31
women 11, 59, 60
Woodstock 72
Worshipful Brother 139
Worshipful Master 125, 127, 128, 129-30, 138-39

Wren, Sir Christopher 42, 45, 99

York Assembly (926 AD) 34
York Minster 31
York Rite 11, 55, 65, 199-200, 200
Yves de Faillon (aka Hugues de Payens) 84

Zerubbabel 25